I LOVE IT HERE

WORKBOOK

I LOVE

CLINT PULVER

IT HERE

WORKBOOK

HOW GREAT LEADERS
CREATE ORGANIZATIONS
THEIR PEOPLE
NEVER WANT TO LEAVE

● ●

PAGE TWO

Cataloguing in publication information
is available from Library and Archives Canada.
ISBN 978-1-77458-337-1 (paperback)

Page Two
pagetwo.com

Proofread by Alison Strobel
Cover design by Peter Cocking
Interior design by Fiona Lee

clintpulver.com

CONTENTS

I.1
INTRODUCTION

WELCOME TO the Management Masterclass Series and Workbook experience! In this fifty-two-video series, you'll learn step-by-step how to bring out the best in your people—and in yourself—as a leader, regardless of what industry you work in. You'll find surprising strategies and exclusive challenges that will change the way you understand leadership and connection, allowing you to connect with your people in a way that truly helps them not only engage in their work but discover their own most valuable skills. If there is one thing you remember from this process, I hope it is this: true mentorship is best achieved one-to-one. That is why, in each section of this workbook, you will find another type of 1-2-1 to help you master each concept presented to you with its coinciding Masterclass video: 1 big idea, 2 insights from our workplace research through the Undercover Millennial program, and 1 moment to master.

There's an old saying that goes, "the faintest ink is more powerful than the strongest memory." Use this workbook intentionally. Write down your thoughts and impressions, your frustrations and your moments of clarity. Record the journey you are experiencing, and reference it often. By doing so, you will gain and retain the tools to become a powerful and influential mentor. I've said it before and I'll say it again—it's not about being the best *in* the world... it's about being the best *for* the world. Use this workbook to rise to the challenge of becoming the best for those you lead, and soon, your employees will truly be saying, "I love it here" for years to come.

All my best,

BECOMING THE MENTOR MANAGER

1.1
WHAT IS A MENTOR MANAGER?

How to assess your leadership on
the standards–connection spectrum

1 big idea

You can take the role of boss, but *mentor* is a title you can't just give yourself. Your people are the only ones who can decide if you're their mentor. It might be a two-way relationship, but it always starts with you—and what development you can offer them.

2 insights from our workplace research

1. The two leadership qualities that have been consistently linked in our research with employees who see their boss as a mentor are *standards* and *connection*. In fact, the presence or absence of these qualities is so determinative that we can actually use them to predict very specific outcomes. Low levels of both and we see disengagement. When a leader has high connection with their employees but does not uphold any standards, we see entitlement. Reverse that—high standards, no connection—and the result in employees is rebellion and pushback.

   But when a leader offers their employees high levels of both? That's mentor management, and that's the sweet spot. In our research, it's the Mentor Managers who have earned the lowest levels of turnover and the highest levels of employee respect. And not just for their leaders—for their organization, their team, and their customers, too.

2. These factors may seem nebulous, but they are actually very easy to identify in managerial practice. *Standards* are your expectations for your employees' behavior and performance on the job. What level of effort or attitude do you hold them to? What do you demand from them in terms of deliverables, benchmarks, quality, punctuality, presence, or client satisfaction?

   Connection, meanwhile, is the level of empathy, recognition, time, and advocacy you are offering your employees. A lack of connection can manifest both physically and emotionally: Are you hard to find? Do you spend a lot of time away from the workplace or behind closed doors? And when your employees do manage to get time from you, are you present for them, or do they feel like you are just ticking boxes?

1 moment to master

This week, I want you to look back at your past leaders and mentors, and use them to assess your own management style on the standards–connection spectrum. Look at the quadrant chart below. You will see the vertical axis is labeled "Standards" and the horizontal axis is labeled "Connection." Up and right are high, down and left are low.

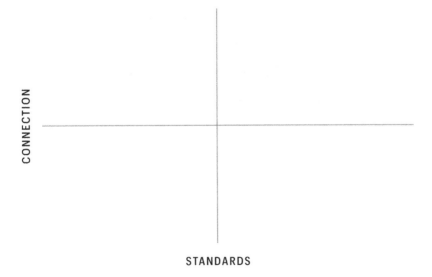

Now, plot your past managers on your spectrum, good and bad. For each "dot," think about who they were as a boss from your perspective as their employee. What level of connection did they offer, and did they offer it as a leader, with the accompanying high expectations, or as buddy, with no standards for your performance at all?

Once you have those relationships in your memory, think about what kind of impact each boss had on your own levels of respect, professional growth, and investment in your job. Then, look at each dot—each manager—and think about this: How much of their style do you see in yourself? Where would you fall on the grid in relation to them? And, most importantly, who do you want to move closer to (or further from) on that spectrum, and what can you change in your style to make that happen?

Mark your own place on your chart, date it, and make a note in your calendar to repeat this exercise six months from now—and every six months thereafter.

1.2
THE 5 Cs OF
GREAT MENTORSHIP

Powerful leadership qualities that
all managers need for success

1 big idea

You can't become a true mentor until the people you are mentoring invite you into their heart.

2 insights from our workplace research

1. Leadership is a two-way street. If you want your employees to learn from you, you have to embody the characteristics that allow them to actively *choose* you. From our interviews with thousands of employees, we can sum up what they look for in a leader in five words: confidence, credibility, competence, candor, and caring.

2. The amazing thing about these five qualities is that none is innate— all of them can be learned! We have witnessed incredible changes when managers who were once getting mediocre results started making the effort to incorporate these attributes into their leadership. It's exponential: the more you lean in to your role as a mentor, the more your employees feel empowered to lean in to their mission and their work.

1 moment to master

This week, choose just one of these qualities and take one step to incorporate more of it into your leadership. Make your choice from your employees' perspective: Which attribute would make the biggest difference to them, right now, if you expanded its role in your leadership today?

Once you've made your choice, here are some ideas for where you could start expanding your abilities.

Confidence: You build confidence by getting out of your own head. The more attention you spend on your employees and their best interests, the less time you'll spend second-guessing yourself.

Credibility: What degree or certification could you earn that would literally *qualify* you to train others?

Competence: Do you need to increase your business acumen? Is the terminology or are the tools your employees use unfamiliar to you? Put away the books and get your hands dirty in the skills your industry demands.

Candor: This one can be tricky—the last thing you want to encourage is tactlessness. Focus on developing *candor with care*: even when you offer difficult feedback, the employee should always feel like you are on their side.

Caring: Give your employees the respect of seeing them as individuals. Listen to their ideas and ambitions. If you're feeling jaded or disconnected, consider taking a course on servant leadership to refresh yourself on your mission.

Pick one quality, take one action, and build out your full "5 Cs" of great mentorship from there.

1.3

THE #1 REASON YOUR STAFF DOESN'T TRUST YOU

VIDEO 4

Why you need to flip your script on loyalty

1 big idea

Everyone wants employees they can trust. But you can't expect loyalty from your people if you haven't earned their trust yourself.

2 insights from our workplace research

1. The employees we've interviewed who loved where they work and felt loyalty to their employer *all* trusted their managers. They knew they could ask for help in a crisis, express a complaint, offer an opinion or idea—always with full faith that they would not be punished for it somewhere down the line. That sense of trust released them from the weight of anxiety or resentment, freeing them to grow and develop, perform at their best, and give their all to their jobs—without ending up feeling like they were on the losing side of a trade.

2. Trust isn't earned through grand gestures, and it's not earned by trying to be everyone's best buddy. When we ask happy employees what their boss did to win their loyalty, what they describe are small, everyday actions that seem so subtle but make a huge impact. An offer of heartfelt thanks for a job well done. A surprise team lunch to celebrate a win or eulogize a failed but exciting project.

A phone call to check in during a crisis. I call these "designed moments," and each one is like a little deposit in a bank account of trust. And, just like with a bank account, when those deposits start to add up to something with true worth, you can ask for more in return. Loyalty, it turns out, pays a nice interest rate.

1 moment to master

This week, pick one employee who seems a bit disconnected from their job and try to design a moment that will have meaning for that specific person. For this to work, it *must* be personalized, so take your time to think about who they are, and don't default to what would make you happy if you were them. Ideally, your designed moment will show that you've been paying attention to what's going on in their life or career. Is there big event on the horizon you could celebrate—a new baby, a graduation, something they've accomplished at work? Is there a special skill or talent you could recognize that would make them feel seen and valued?

If you don't get the reaction you were hoping for, don't lose heart. Think about how they received your moment, and try to design the next one in a way that's more suited to their personality. All you're doing, in essence, is being *there* for your employees, literally and emotionally. Keep your moments subtle, keep them considerate, and keep them coming—and that presence will start to pay all kinds of dividends.

1.4

CAN MENTORS MAKE MONEY?

VIDEO 5

The link between your people and your profit

1 big idea

A good business doesn't flow from good money. Good money flows from a good business.

2 insights from our workplace research

1. Employees who don't love where they work will undermine your product, your culture, and your relationship with your customers—not because they *want* to, but because they can't function at their best. When we look at workplaces where the leaders are not paying attention to their people—each individual's interests, goals, ideal placement, and career growth—we don't just see damaging turnover, we also see a lack of innovation, productivity, and caring customer service. Guess what happens to the profits then?

    And it's not just our researchers who've noticed this link. A recent Gallup study[1] showed that disengaged employees cost their companies an additional 18% of their pay—assuming an average salary of $50,000, that's $9,000 *per year* for every employee on your team who is not connecting with their work.

2. That same Gallup study also found that a full two-thirds of the global workforce is currently disengaged. That's a lot of edge to gain with a little mentor management! As a leader, if you can work on becoming more *people-driven* and less *entity-driven*, you'll

inspire a better culture of performance that will help you stand out from your competitors. As you invest more in your people, they'll invest more in creating and delivering your products and services—and the bottom-line results will reveal themselves. It's a simple, straight road: good mentorship, good people, good product, good profit.

1 moment to master

This week, try shifting your focus from your *company* as a profit machine to your *people* as the engine of that machine.

Do this by adding one factor to your quarterly metrics: the short-term personal and professional goals of your employees. Talk to your people, and find out what each would like to achieve over the next six months, and over the next five years. (If they don't know, this is a great opportunity to help them find out.) Then, record those goals, and make them as much or more of a priority as boosting your sales, increasing your output, or reducing your overhead. Do this with a genuine heart, and with commitment and integrity, and, over time, you'll start seeing returns in loyalty and the drive for excellence. And, trust me—the profit will follow.

1.5

ARE YOUR EMPLOYEES EXISTING OR LIVING?

VIDEO 6

The 3 fundamentals of a fulfilling workplace

1 big idea

As a leader, you are the factor that determines whether your employees are *living* their lives at work, or simply *existing*.

To truly live, every human needs the "3 Ps" of a fulfilling life: purpose, passion, and the ability to provide. Without them, your employees are not growing, not engaging, not *living*. They need more, and as an employer, it's up to you to provide it.

2 insights from our workplace research

1. The three fundamentals of living aren't magic—they're process. The leaders we've met who achieve real engagement deliver these seemingly spiritual concepts in a very practical way:

   Purpose: They provide a vision of something bigger—who they help, why it matters, and how they can make a difference every day.

   Passion: They help each employee work to their strengths, and help them grow those strengths with incremental challenges.

   The ability to provide: This one's simple—they pay a competitive wage for their region and market.

2. Great leaders make the "3 Ps" part of their workplace culture. How do they do this? By *listening*. Are your people stressed? Are they getting what they need? If they're anxious or lost, what could you do to get them back to feeling present and alive?

1 moment to master

This week, make a list of every employee on your team and write down one key strength for each of them. Next to that, write down one role or pathway at your organization where that specific employee could best use their individual strength. Is everyone in the best position to access the three fundamentals of living? If not, what can you do to start moving them closer?

If you can't name a strength for each employee, that's a sign you should pay attention to. It means it's time to invest more deeply in getting to know your people.

1.6

DID YOU KNOW
THAT MANAGERS CAN
TIME TRAVEL?

VIDEO 7

How reaching out to the past can
prepare you for your future

1 big idea

Stop trying to "be the mentor you wish you had." Instead, try to be
the mentor you were lucky enough to actually have.

2 insights from our workplace research

1. Creating a fictional role model is a nice idea, but it ignores a more
   meaningful truth. Most of us did have at least one great mentor,
   somewhere along the line. Honoring that relationship has great
   power, and refusing to acknowledge it can doom you to forget the
   lessons they taught you.

2. Offering gratitude for your past mentors is like tapping into that
   same well of mentorship all over again. We've seen incredible outcomes from leaders who looked up past mentors online or through
   an old workplace, or who even simply wrote a letter to thank someone long gone, with no intention of actually sending it. Creating
   those words of thanks can be like setting a goal for yourself to
   embody those lessons for the next generation.

1 moment to master

This week, take the time to mentally acknowledge your past mentors. Think about the leaders and guides from your past who had a positive impact on your work and life—whether that's a teacher, a boss, a co-worker, a family member, or even a friend you admired. What are the links between who they were for you then, and who you are for the people you lead today?

Now, call that past mentor forward in your mind as if they were still your mentor, and consider some of your leadership decisions and actions from their perspective. If that person from your past were here today, how might that affect the leader you are becoming? This simple exercise can be a way to bring that important person along with you on your own mentorship journey going forward.

MANAGEMENT MASTERCLASS SELF-ASSESSMENT

**Module Review:
Mastering Your Moments Video 1**

SECTION 1

Becoming the Mentor Manager

Part 1: Quiz

1. What are the four types of management styles, as measured on the standards–connection spectrum?

   1. _____

   2. _____

   3. _____

   4. _____

2. What is the term for a deliberate, personalized act of care intended to build a "bank account" of loyalty and trust with an individual employee?

   A _____ moment

3. List the five qualities of great mentorship (*hint: they all start with "C"*).

    I. _____

    2. _____

    3. _____

    4. _____

    5. _____

4. The Wright Brothers and the air travel empire they built are an example of how:

    a) Good business flows from having good access to capital

    b) Good growth flows from taking physical and economic risks

    c) Good money flows from establishing a good business run by people who have passion

    d) Good engineering flows from mechanical failures

5. What are the "3 Ps" of a fulfilling life?

    I. _____

    2. _____

    3. _____

6. Who is the best person to inspire your mentorship style?

    a) The mentor you wish you had

    b) Yoda from *Star Wars*

    c) Mr. Jensen

    d) The mentor you actually had

Part 1: Answers

1. The Buddy Manager, the Controlling Manager, the Removed Manager, the Mentor Manager (see lesson 1.1)

2. A designed moment (see lesson 1.3)

3. Confidence, credibility, competence, candor, caring (see lesson 1.2)

4. C: Good money flows from establishing a good business run by people who have passion (see lesson 1.4)

5. Purpose, passion, and the ability to provide (see lesson 1.5)

6. D: The mentor you actually had (see lesson 1.6)

Part 2: "Mastering Your Moments" Checklist

By the end of this section, I have:

1. Reviewed the standards–connection spectrum quadrant chart (high to low standards; high to low connection) and plotted out the most memorable managers I have had in my own life.

   GO DEEPER:

   ☐ What did you learn from this exercise about how your level of standards and connection can affect the way you lead?

   _____

   _____

   _____

   ☐ If you haven't done so yet, turn to page 5 and plot your own management style now. Add a reminder in your calendar six months from now to repeat this exercise.

2. Chosen one quality from the "5 Cs" of great mentorship to focus on developing in myself.

GO DEEPER:

- [ ] Which quality have you chosen to work on first, and why?
- [ ] What actions have you taken to strengthen that quality?
- [ ] What quality do you plan to work on next?

3. Designed a personalized, meaningful moment for one employee that will strengthen the level of trust and connection between us.

GO DEEPER:

☐ Describe that moment.

☐ What was the result?

_____

_____

_____

_____

_____

_____

_____

_____

_____

_____

_____

_____

4. Asked each member of my team what their short-term goals are for this quarter.

GO DEEPER:

☐ How has this exercise affected way you approach your company's immediate goals?

☐ What are your own immediate, short-term goals?

5. Made a list of the key strengths of each member of my team, and identified the role or department that would best suit their strengths.

GO DEEPER:

☐ Has this exercise revealed any changes that would benefit your team?

☐ How do you plan to execute those changes?

☐ How do you plan to measure or assess the results?

6. Meditated on my past influences and mentors, and how they helped me become who I am today.

GO DEEPER:

- [ ] Have you reached out to offer your thanks to a past mentor?
- [ ] How did that experience feel?
- [ ] Has that conversation led to any immediate impacts? What are they?

— 2 —

CREATING YOUR DREAM TEAM

2.1

WHAT *SPACE JAM* CAN TEACH YOU ABOUT HIRING

VIDEO 8

The foundations of creating a Dream Team

1 big idea

Every manager hears about "hiring the right people." But how can you hire the right people if you don't know who they are?

2 insights from our workplace research

1. The best way to define your ideal employees is to visualize them first. What values, skills, talents, and attitudes do they have? Be specific, and picture them actually in your space: meeting, collaborating, completing their tasks, selling your products—whatever it is you need them to do. Throw in a stressful day, an unexpected setback, the celebration of a win. How would your dream employees handle each of these moments? Who are they as individuals, and as teammates?

2. Never let a short-term need control your long-term success. We see it all the time in our research: a manager is badly understaffed and needs a warm body on the floor, so they hire someone who seems good enough. But while an occasional bad hire might not seem like a big deal, bringing the wrong person onto a team is like snipping one thread in the fabric of your workplace culture. Sooner or later, the whole thing starts to unravel. So hold the line, and hire right.

1 moment to master

Take a moment to visualize your ideal employees working in the ideal workspace. What specific words would you use to describe these employees' traits? Focused? Friendly? Driven? Competitive? Empathetic? Assertive? Easygoing? Whatever feels right, write it down below.

Once you have about six traits, take a look at your list. Guess what you have? A Dream Team shopping list. Post that piece of paper where you can see it every day, embody those traits yourself, and do everything you can to encourage and reward them in your existing staff. And don't hire *anybody* who doesn't fit your list. Remember: it's all about the right person, the right fit, and the right placement.

2.2

HOW TO HIRE FOR "RIGHT," NOT FOR "RIGHT NOW"

1 big idea

How can you stop a short-term staffing crunch from hurting your long-term success? You do it with three magic words:

Always.

Be.

Recruiting.

2 insights from our workplace research

1. The most innovative organizations we come across in our research are always *proactive*. When faced with a sudden vacancy or a spike in production, most managers will scramble to recruit the first warm bodies they can find. But leaders with vision will never let a staffing crisis put their workplace culture at risk.

   What do they do instead? They constantly look for good employees, even when they don't need to hire. The managers we've worked with who maintain a productive culture are always accepting résumés, fostering relationships with good people they meet in their industry, and running referral programs to tap into the networks of their best employees. Then, when it comes time to turn on the hiring tap, the right candidates are there.

2. An "always be recruiting" mindset isn't just about keeping a faithful eye outward. It also requires you to be aware of what a candidate sees when they look at you. Do you have an easy-to-find careers page on your website—and, if you do, does it read like a "sorry, no vacancy" sign, or is it a friendly window into who you are and what you offer? And how welcoming, accessible, and visible is your team culture? Effective recruiting doesn't stop at a compelling job posting: it's how you present yourself and your business in your social media feeds, at events, on LinkedIn, and even in the feeling and design of your workspace ... all the time.

1 moment to master

This week, conduct an audit of how your business is presenting itself to potential recruits—even if you have no immediate plans to hire. If a talented person came across your website today, how likely would they be to reach out? What would your workspace and team culture look like to an outsider who walked in, and what are you doing to maintain relationships with great people you meet in your industry and beyond? Finally, what kind of rewards and programs do you have in place to encourage your employees to recommend you to their friends?

Look at what you're doing, analyze the results, and think about what you could change to be more proactive in your hiring. And then never roll the dice on being *reactive* again.

2.3

DO YOU KNOW YOUR HIRING ABCs?

VIDEO 10

The 3 qualities you must look for in a job candidate

1 big idea

There's only one concrete qualification a manager can know about a candidate from reading their résumé.

What is it? It's how good that person is at putting together a résumé.

2 insights from our workplace research

1. Leaders often fall into two camps when hiring: A) "I need to tick all of these experience and certification boxes," or B) "I go with my gut." But the hiring market is changing, and we've seen each of these approaches lead managers to miss out on spotting big potential talent—and big red flags.

   So what should a leader look for? Start with your ABCs: attitude, behavior, and character. Don't just email those references—*call* them, have a real conversation, and listen carefully to what they say (and don't say). And with more than a third[2] of candidates admitting to lying on their résumé, make sure to do a background check on the credentials they list. Some candidates might consider a white lie or two to be simple "self-marketing," but it can actually tell you a lot about their values, and their willingness to cut corners.

2. If you really want to know if a candidate will benefit your team, why not involve that team in the hiring process? The people who will be working alongside your new hire know better than anyone what needs doing and the attitude and abilities it takes to do it. Have an employee who will be working directly with the new hire sit in on at least one of the interviews, and listen to what they have to say when it's over. This strategy can be a double win: you'll get smart feedback from someone who knows what they're talking about, and you'll also be showing your existing employee that their opinion is valued.

1 moment to master

This week, take some time to reflect on the last few people you hired, and the factors that led you to hire them. Were you going by gut instinct, or by the credentials on paper? Or did you also assess them for the "ABCs" of attitude, behavior, and character?

Once you've examined your process, weigh that level of effort against the end result of your decision. How did those candidates perform? Did they stay? Are they adding value to your team, or do you still have questions about their fit? Regularly looking back like this to connect the dots between your hiring process and the outcomes of those hires will help you identify important trends and habits in your decision-making—both the strategies that work, and the gaps you need to address.

2.4
ARE YOU IGNORING A GOLD MINE?

VIDEO 11

The unsung value of hiring internally

1 big idea

Here's something we hear all the time: "Our company's greatest resource is our people."

But hey—if that's true, why do so many leaders automatically hire outsiders when a management position comes up? If a workforce is a resource, too many companies see it as a quarry—disposable, replaceable rocks and gravel. Instead, try seeing it for what it really is: a *gold mine*.

2 insights from our workplace research

1. Continually hiring from outside when good positions come up in your company has two interconnected effects: First, it tells your entire staff that there is no place for them to grow within your company, so they become discouraged. Second, once that realization sets in, the result is critical levels of disengagement. Stacking your mid-range positions with younger or less experienced outsiders might seem like a way to save money right now, but it will hurt you in the long run when you're dealing with high turnover and low productivity. Consider this fact alone: the average cost of replacing an employee is currently sitting at around $15,000.[3]

2. On the flipside, we've seen that regularly promoting your people from within delivers higher levels of engagement, a more cohesive work culture, and much, much lower turnover. (And why wouldn't it, when people know they're working in a company that values them?) Internal promotion has a practical value, too: an existing employee *already has* the co-worker and customer relationships a new hire would need to spend weeks developing, *already has* a good knowledge of your culture and internal practices, *already has* a foundation of loyalty—from day one in their new position.

1 moment to master

This week, look ahead to any openings that might potentially come up in your organization over the next year or so—even if only theoretically. Now think: Who in your company might have the potential to eventually be promoted in that direction? And what could you do *now* to help them build the skills they'll need for that role when it does become available?

Offering that employee opportunities for incremental development—starting today—will benefit you both: they'll earn more skills and feel more supported in their career growth, and, if and when that job does open up, you won't have to cold-start an employee who isn't prepared for more responsibility. Try it out, and see what a difference it can make when your people feel like they're working in a place with a future.

2.5

HOW TO KNOW WHO YOU'RE REALLY HIRING

The 3 most revealing questions you can ask a candidate

1 big idea

Mentorship doesn't need to start on your employee's first day on the job. If you're doing it right, it starts before you even say "you're hired."

2 insights from our workplace research

1. Too many job interviews go like this: the manager tries to impress with clever, trendy interview questions, and the candidate tries to impress with well-practiced answers (often derived from researching those same trendy questions). What you each end up learning is that you're both good at mastering interview techniques. What you won't learn, however, is what you'll need from each other in your working relationship, and if those needs fit together.

2. To find out who a candidate really is and what they really want (and vice versa), you need to have an authentic conversation. Think that's something you can't control, or that depends on the personality of the interviewee? Try following the lead of a chain of medical clinics we researched that was the best at this we've ever seen— resulting in an average annual employee retention rate of more than 70%. The hiring manager always asked open-ended questions that weren't designed to *test*, but instead to *understand*, like:

- "What factors would be on the list of your ideal job?"

- "Tell me about a past job where you wish things had been different."

- "Who is someone that you loved working with?"

Questions like these aren't about making the candidate prove themselves, they're about learning whether that person can thrive in your environment—and if you'll thrive with them.

1 moment to master

This week, think back to the last few interviews you held. What kinds conversations did you have? Did they feel authentic, or were they mostly a practiced back-and-forth? Next, think about the candidates you ended up choosing. Did you each fully understand what the others' needs were, or did one or both of you end up feeling like it was a bad fit?

Once you've analyzed your past results, think about changing up the game for your next interview. Consider a few open-ended questions that might reveal more about who a candidate is—not to judge or rank them, but to get a better sense of their needs, and how (or if) you can meet them. That's mentorship at its best—right from before your employee is even your employee.

2.6

THE #1 THING YOU'RE GETTING WRONG ABOUT DISABILITY

Why inclusion is so important in your organization

1 big idea

Everybody has disabilities. Everybody! We all have things we're really good at, and we all have stuff we can't do very well—and that includes your existing employees, every candidate you interview, your boss, me—and you as well.

2 insights from our workplace research

1. Great leaders put aside assumptions and learn to recognize value. Once you understand that each one of us has unique talents—and unique barriers—you can start to see the entire spectrum of possibility that each individual could bring to your company.

2. When managers we've worked with made the choice to widen the range of ability on their team, an amazing change often took place. Their workplaces gained a palpable and powerful spirit of positivity and cohesiveness that uplifted the whole team, along with everyone who came into their business.

   We've seen the addition of new experiences and perspectives crack open an uninspired or unproductive culture, leading to something more creative, and more effective.

1 moment to master

This week, take one step to learn what local supports are around to help you invite more diversity into your workplace. Start by visiting DOL.gov (or your own country's labor department) and search under topics for disability resources. In the U.S., you'll find initiatives for locating candidates, guidance on interviewing and onboarding, and even some tax credits that could help with any adjustments you might need to make.

When you're ready to take the next step, try launching an internship, or connect with AskJAN.org or your local disability employment center. There's a lot of potential waiting out there, so open the door, and start re-thinking your idea of who really benefits from inclusive practices.

2.7

HAVE YOU PUT THE DOG LOVERS IN CHARGE OF THE SNAKES?

3 commonsense questions that help employees thrive

1 big idea

If you aren't curious about your employees, how can you know if they're in the right position?

Think about it this way: if you ran a pet store, who would you want taking care of your reptile department? The employee who only loves dogs, or the one who's a big fan of snakes?

2 insights from our workplace research

1. As odd as it sounds, this analogy is not hypothetical—this comes from real-world research we did at a successful and growing chain of pet stores. Every employee there had been placed according to their interests and passions: the tropical fish hobbyist was taking care of the aquariums, the cat fancier was over with the scratching posts and teaser toys. It sounds like common sense, but—so, so often!—this simplicity gets lost in the blur to hire and fill shifts. But when your customers go looking for advice and expertise only to get a shrug (or worse, bad advice) you won't be having to struggle to fill shifts for long, because those customers will go somewhere else.

2. Knowing where your people can work at their best starts with curiosity: getting to know who they are, what they want, and what they like to do in their spare time. So, talk to them! Ask them about their passions, talents, and hobbies; about where they want to go in their work and in their larger life. Step gently, keep your questions open-ended, and try not to jump in with your own thoughts and ideas. Give your employees your attention and plenty of space to talk, and you'll be surprised by how eager they are to step into that light and show you more about themselves.

1 moment to master

This week, carve out some time for each of your direct employees and ask them three specific questions:

1. "What's your life's dream?"
2. "What do you most want to achieve in your life?"
3. "What means the most to you?"

These might feel a bit personal, so try to keep the conversation as a chat and not an interrogation. If they seem reluctant or unwilling to share at this point, don't push. The goal is not to cross boundaries, but simply to communicate interest in your team. Over time—and with consistent, small displays of care and attention—that trust will build, and you'll find out what you need to know to place each of your employees where they can shine.

2.8

YOU CAN'T FORCE FUN—
BUT YOU CAN DESIGN IT

VIDEO 15

_____

**5 ways to plan a team-building
experience that actually builds your team**

1 big idea

A team-building experience doesn't have to be hokey, cliquey, or aggressively "fun." The trick is to create an event that's an *extension of* (not a *replacement for*) your ongoing efforts to build connection.

2 insights from our workplace research

1. The most fundamental ingredient of a successful team-building experience is to meet your people where they are. If your team culture is serious and formal, don't infantilize your employees with toys or children's play. Do your people tend to be soft-spoken with each other? Don't force them into conflict with war games. You may think you're doing your employees a favor by pushing them out of their comfort zone, but look at it this way: If your intent is to make each person feel like they're an important part of the team, why put them in a situation where they feel alienated and misunderstood? Designing an inclusive event that's suited to your culture shows your employees that you care, and that you're paying attention.

2. The best team experiences we've witnessed let every participant contribute in their own way. Think escape rooms or quiz nights, where everyone brings their own unique set of knowledge or

skills, and where a win for the team is a win for everyone. Or, consider "social" sports—like ax throwing, bowling, ping-pong, lawn games—these types of events allow different personality types to choose how they get involved: play to win, play for fun, step in and out, or hang back and watch.

1 moment to master

A team experience doesn't have to be a big weekend outing—you can design these types of moments on any regular day. This week, see if you can give your employees one quick, unexpected experience that will shake them out of their daily grind and get them talking to each other in a new way.

How about clearing some space on a wall and asking everyone to start contributing sticky notes with a great office memory written on them? Is there a big sports or other televised event coming up that you could all watch together in the break room? Or what about an impromptu walking tour of your local neighborhood? (You'd be surprised what people start noticing about their surroundings when you break them out of their daily groove.)

Whatever you choose, make it fun, make it inclusive, and make sure it's suited to who your people really are—not who you want to push them to become.

MANAGEMENT MASTERCLASS SELF-ASSESSMENT

**Module Review:
Mastering Your Moments Video 2**

SECTION 2

Creating Your Dream Team

Part 1: Quiz

1. Along with hiring internally when possible, what three other factors are critical for effective hiring?

   a) The right person, the right salary range, and the right references

   b) The right person, the right skills, and the right attitude

   c) The right person, the right fit, and the right placement

   d) The right person, the right IQ, and the right connections

2. What are the "ABCs" you should be looking for when interviewing a new job candidate?

   1. _____

   2. _____

   3. _____

3. If the first two of the three most effective interview questions for revealing a candidate's personality are these:

What factors would be on the list of your ideal job?

and

Tell me about a past job where you wish things had been different.

Then what is the third?

_____

_____

4. What two impacts can start to develop in your team if you consistently hire from outside your company?

a) Ambition and loyalty

b) Discouragement and disengagement

c) Competition and aggression

d) Obedience and respect

5. To design a Dream Team, a manager must remember these three words:

a) Attract, Bargain, Renegotiate

b) Ask for Better References

c) Avoid Bringing on Relatives

d) Always Be Recruiting

6. Name two of the five elements of a successful team-building experience named in this section.

I. _____

2. _____

7. True or false: In the U.S., people with disabilities tend to require more sick days than people who do not have disabilities.

☐ True
☐ False

8. If you were running a pet store, which employee should you put in charge of the snakes?

a) The person who is allergic to dogs, so they don't get sick

b) Someone who doesn't like snakes, so they aren't tempted to coddle them

c) The snake lover, because they will be more knowledgeable and engaged

d) The person with the fewest number of phobias

Part 1: Answers

1. C: The right person, the right fit, and the right placement (see lesson 2.1)

2. Attitude, behavior, and character (see lesson 2.3)

3. "Who is someone that you loved working with?" (see lesson 2.5)

4. B: Discouragement and disengagement (see lesson 2.4)

5. D: Always Be Recruiting (see lesson 2.2)

6. Any of: A sense of achievement; meeting people where they are; fun, not fighting; customization; opportunity to give back (see lesson 2.8)

7. False: Studies show that people with disabilities take fewer sick days (see lesson 2.6)

8. C: The snake lover, because they will be more knowledgeable and engaged (see lesson 2.7)

Part 2: "Mastering Your Moments" Checklist

By the end of this section, I have:

1. Taken the time to visualize my Dream Team: who I want working for me, what they would look like in action, and how they would behave with their team.

   GO DEEPER:

   ☐ Have you created your "Dream Team shopping list" by naming at least six specific qualities you want in your team?

   ☐ List those qualities and why they are important to you now:

   _____

   _____

   _____

   _____

   _____

   _____

   _____

   _____

   _____

   _____

2. Conducted an "audit" of how welcoming my company is to potential recruits, including our website and careers page, our visible workplace culture, and how we interact with our larger network.

GO DEEPER:

☐ How would an outsider describe your workplace culture based on what they can see from your public-facing workspaces and content?

3. Considered the outcomes of the last three or so people I hired, and analyzed their hiring process.

GO DEEPER:

☐ How much time and effort did you put into checking backgrounds and interviewing references?

☐ What trends or blind spots have you discovered in your hiring practices?

4. Taken a closer look at my existing team for promotion or leadership potential.

GO DEEPER:

☐ What kind of established career paths exist in your company?

☐ If there aren't many, what could you do to create more opportunities for professional development and advancement?

5. Made a list of the questions I have asked in my last three or four interviews with a job candidate.

GO DEEPER:

☐ Did the candidates' later performance and personality match up with their original responses?

☐ What new questions could I ask that might help close such gaps?

6. Made a list of possible events or experiences I could create to help bring my team together.

GO DEEPER:

☐ What kind of team experiences have you created for your employees in the past?

☐ Did the experience help your team connect with each other and with their job in a positive way?

☐ Why or why not?

_____

_____

_____

_____

_____

_____

_____

_____

_____

_____

_____

_____

7. Visited DOL.gov and AskJAN.org to learn about assistance with and opportunities for hiring people with disabilities at my organization.

GO DEEPER:

☐ How much diversity exists on your current team?

☐ What assumptions and habits might be leading to you hire mostly the same types of people?

☐ What could a wider range of experiences bring to your team, and to the performance of your company?

8. Invested additional time into getting to know my individual employees, including non-work-related information like hobbies.

GO DEEPER:

- [ ] What special knowledge or hidden talents have you uncovered that you didn't know about before?

- [ ] How could these interests and abilities add value to your team?

— 3 —

HOW TO EARN "I LOVE IT HERE"

3.1

THE #1 REASON YOUR EMPLOYEES QUIT

Why you need to understand the true cost of turnover

1 big idea

As a leader, you are either the number one reason your people stay, or the number one reason they quit.

2 insights from our workplace research

1. When we go undercover and ask burned-out employees why they're thinking about quitting, the conversation usually starts with the typical answers: they're looking for better pay, different hours, a shorter commute, and so on. But continue the conversation past those surface-level needs, and the same factor always reveals itself: *leadership*—or a lack of it.

   Over 75% of the organizational turnover we've examined can be traced back to inconsistent management, micromanagement, too much criticism, or not enough caring. On average, more than half of the employees we interview in cultures like these are ready to bounce the *moment* something better comes along. But when we find the opposite? Pay, hours, commuting time—all of these "typical" employment problems become minor issues in comparison to staying in a workplace that works.

2. If you don't understand why your people are leaving, you won't know what you need to change to entice them to stay. But simply by paying attention—on an ongoing basis, every day—you

will come to learn whether or not your employees feel like they're growing. Whether or not they feel like they're in the right position. If they feel undervalued or overworked or underpaid. That gives you the power to make changes, and to become a company where they *want* to work, grow, and contribute.

1 moment to master

Take a moment this week to think about the last time one of your employees quit. Was it expected, or was it a surprise? If it was expected, what could you have changed about how you communicated with that employee that might have created a different outcome? Even better, what could you have done *from the moment they were hired* that might have changed the result?

If it was a surprise, think about *why*. Do you need to improve your awareness? What conversations could you start having with your people that might alert you to the risk of them leaving?

Remember, if your employees don't feel seen and valued, they *will* go somewhere else. Your job as a leader is to keep reminding them—through actions, not words—about all the reasons they should stay.

3.2
STOP TRYING TO OUTSOURCE HAPPINESS

VIDEO 17

How to know when it's time to hire a retention specialist

1 big idea

Every employee in your organization deserves to feel like someone on their leadership team knows their name. If that person isn't you, who is it?

2 insights from our workplace research

1. There's one moment that always arrives in every fast-growing company we've worked with: the leader looks out over the floor and realizes, for the first time, that they don't recognize an employee's face.

   It can be weird for a hands-on leader to accept that one-on-one management just isn't possible anymore, but it's simple math. If you used to have half a dozen employees but now you have 50, 100, 150-plus, you simply can't truly know every one of them: their hobbies, what they're good at, where they need development, what goals they want to meet. But the mistake many leaders make at this moment is to believe that outsourcing their HR can solve this problem. Sure, you can offload admin like payroll, but you can't outsource recognition, development, purpose, *happiness*. These principles need to be delivered directly.

2. If you've reached the point where you're losing track of your employees, it's time to put an employee retention specialist on your team. We've seen this work beautifully in so many companies: while senior management guides and models the overall workplace culture, your retention specialist builds mentorship networks, creates and manages merit programs, conducts regular status interviews, and makes sure that each employee feels recognized, supported in their career development, and, in a word, *seen*. Having someone on your team whose specific role is employee retention is the absolute best way to maintain a consistent level of engagement and to keep your people connected to their purpose—and connected to your company, too.

1 moment to master

This week, think about all the people on your workforce, and whether each of them has a direct relationship with someone on your leadership team who knows their name, talents, interests, and goals. If you can't join those dots, it's time to hire or appoint an employee retention specialist.

If you have the size and means this could easily be a full-time position, one that may even pay for itself in reduced turnover. If you don't, find that one person on your team who is really good at relationships, give them a raise and access to training in the principles of mentor management, then officially add employee retention to their role. You'll be giving your employees the support and attention they need, while taking someone's potential for caring and turning it into a meaningful career in your company—and that's a double win.

3.3

THE BIGGEST CONVERSATION YOU LOVE TO AVOID

VIDEO 18

How to talk to your employees about money

1 big idea

Never be afraid to face those inevitable conversations about money and raises—no matter how awkward they can feel. Each and every one is an opportunity for you to step up as an advocate.

2 insights from our workplace research

1. In our research we often hear frustration from leaders about staff trying to jump the seniority queue—say, asking for a big raise after just a few weeks on the job. But those requests don't have to be a problem—they're actually your chance to take on the role of coach and say, "Okay, I hear you. Now let's figure out what we can do together to get you that level."

   Get a figure on paper, so you can lay out exactly what's needed for them to reach that income: more skills, more responsibilities, even a specific number of hours. Then, work with that employee to create the development plan that will take them there.

2. There are stark realities in small business, and sometimes a leader just can't give more. The job then is to figure out what other kinds of value you could offer to acknowledge that employee's worth. Maybe it's more vacation days, support with furthering an

educational goal, allowances for more telecommuting or flex time, or something else entirely. Honest talk about what they actually need and want—beyond money—can help you deepen the relationship you've been working to build as a mentor.

1 moment to master

This week, think of the employees on your team who are really adding value to your company, and ask yourself honestly what kind of value you're offering them in return. What could you do to increase that reward, through a raise, or something else that could help them meet their needs? And if they haven't yet ticked the boxes to officially earn a raise, what kind of advocacy can you offer to help move them forward into better moneymaking potential?

Even if you're a tiny operation with no real path to significant career or income growth, this effort can pay off hugely for both you and your employees. Put your discomfort with money talk aside and be willing to get real about value, and you could turn a forgettable four-month stint for a young person into a memorable, meaningful two-year job that they'll think back on as an experience that mattered.

3.4

HOW TO MAKE ANYONE FEEL LIKE A MILLION BUCKS

The 7 ways your employees want to be recognized

1 big idea

The world is always telling us that our *work* is what defines our *worth*. It might not be fair, it might not be true, but your employees feel it—every single day.

2 insights from our workplace research

1. As a leader, it's your job to communicate to your employees that they *have* worth, in every way you can. When you recognize a person's value—by showing them that what they do is important— they start to see that value in themselves. We've seen this effort empower employees to give more to their work, simply because they know they have more to give.

2. The absolute best way to spark that million-dollar fire is by rewarding people for what they do. A culture that recognizes value starts with vocal praise—and lots of it. It means literal rewards too, like surprise bonuses (money, gift cards, prizes, food, concert tickets and outings, even extra time off when you see someone go above and beyond). It means showing trust by letting people set their own schedules. And it means having a formal recognition program that gives people the chance to be honored by name in front of their family, their peers, and their entire industry.

1 moment to master

The key pillar of a supportive culture is that vocal praise—but many leaders we meet find it difficult to give, whether out of shyness, misattention, or the misguided idea that praise is "coddling." So this week I want you to make the leap and push past that reticence.

At your next team meeting, take a moment to go around the room and list one unique contribution from each person on your team: a hard push to finish a project, a great idea, even the ability to lift the team's mood in stressful times. It might feel awkward at first, but we've seen that this kind of personalized, visible recognition can be a defining moment for your employees—you're saying in front of everyone: I see you, and *I see your worth.*

3.5

IS "STAYGNATION" KILLING YOUR BUSINESS?

VIDEO 20

The 3 types of burnout—and how to address them

1 big idea

Do you know what's worse than having an employee quit on you? Losing their loyalty and having them *stay*.

When "staygnation" enters your workplace, it can deflate absolutely everything—culture, energy, momentum, results, *everything*. That's why true mentorship sometimes requires coaching people out.

2 insights from our workplace research

1. When we examine a case of company-wide staygnation and start looking for the cause, it almost always leads to the same factor: burnout. That's why it's critical to spot and address burnout as soon as you find it.

   There are *tons* of signs if you know what to look for, but let's start with the top three we see in our research: persistent negativity, persistent procrastination, and persistent apathy. *Persistent* is the key word here: ideally, as a Mentor Manager, you would spot complaining, foot-dragging, or indifference immediately and take steps to turn it around. But when you've done everything you can and the employee still seems disengaged? Now you're dealing with a different level of problem.

2. If you do find yourself faced with one or more of these persistent behaviors in an employee, it isn't necessarily too late. Double down on communication, and get that employee to open up about what's really behind their attitude. Do they need more challenge? Are they afraid of looking like a failure? Are there problems at home, or some bad team dynamics you need to address? Try to talk openly with them to get the deeper issue out in the open, so you can both work on fixing it—or, if you've tried and nothing has worked, so you can help them find a better career fit, within or outside your company.

1 moment to master

This week, think of someone on your team who's been showing signs of burnout. What could you do to help wake them up? Are they overwhelmed? Do they need more challenge or responsibility? Or do you need to deepen your focus to uncover the heart of a bigger problem?

Get those lines of communication open as soon as possible—if you catch it early enough, you may even find that the simple act of showing care and attention can go a long way to re-igniting that flame.

3.6

WHEN IS A DONUT MORE THAN A DONUT?

The secret ingredient for creating
a positive workplace culture

1 big idea

Have you ever looked out at your workforce and wondered why they just can't seem to come together as a team? Well, consider the one person you're leaving out of that picture. That's right: it's *you*.

2 insights from our workplace research

1. A cohesive team culture starts and ends with you. As a leader, it's your responsibility to set a vision for your workplace culture, and to design moments that will guide and foster that vision.

   Here's the amazing thing: those moments can be so small! Take one employee we interviewed a few years back: he told us that what he remembered most about his favorite manager was the way he brought in donuts every Tuesday morning. A simple thing, sure, but the true value was in the time he gave his people on those mornings to gather and chat about their lives and the work ahead while they munched on their crullers and jelly-filleds. Call it "the Donut Principle"—but it's really not about the donuts. It's about creating opportunities for your team to get to know each other as *people*, not just as some kind of traffic they move through from 9 to 5.

2. Okay, yes, on one level it's simple, but (as I'm sure you've guessed) it's more complex and subtle, too. If you want these moments to be *more* than moments—to be building blocks for a cohesive,

high-performance culture—you have to be intentional about *how* your employees are connecting. Participate, quietly facilitate, and model the kind of respect and mutual interest you want to see in your staff. And, most importantly, be clear in your mind about what it is you're trying to create. "I want everyone to get along" is not enough. You need to have a detailed vision in your mind about what kind of workplace you want, whether that's efficient and focused, or lively and fun.

1 moment to master

This week, set that vision for the culture you want by mapping it out. Write down three adjectives to describe your current workplace culture. Is it light-hearted? Stuffy? Competitive? Don't overthink: just go with your gut.

Next, visualize your *ideal* team atmosphere. Picture the actual employees you have on your staff right now: How would you like to see them working together, strategizing, socializing? Write down three words to describe *that* culture.

Now you have a definition of where you are, and a direction for where you want to go. Need a first step? Review both lists and choose the one word that feels most important (what defines "important" in this context is up to you). That word—and the designed moments that will foster that culture—is the Milestone #1 you're aiming for.

3.7

THE TOP 10 PERKS YOUR EMPLOYEES REALLY WANT

VIDEO 22

How to build a benefit package that supercharges retention

1 big idea

Caring, connection, advocacy: if you follow our research, you know how important these factors are in building employee loyalty. But as much as your employees may love where they work, that love can't translate into retention if you aren't pairing your mentorship with a life they can live.

2 insights from our workplace research

1. The companies we've researched that really kill at retention support each employee's existence as a whole, not just the part of it they spend at work. You may not always be able to offer a better paycheck than your competitors, but it's always in your power to offer a better life, along with the sense of security they need to be able to enjoy that life.

   If your people are breaking under the weight of family demands, health issues, emotional stress, or financial anxiety, they won't be able to bring their best selves to their job. Flex time to help with family issues, fitness memberships, counselling and mental health support, adequate vacation time, tuition funding—and, of course, the big one: health and dental benefits—we've seen all of these programs help employees function better at work, because they can function better outside of work.

2. To be effective at boosting retention, workplace benefits have to be reliable. Sure, the employees we've interviewed have always appreciated surprise perks like a sudden afternoon off or a free group lunch, but when they were ready to make long-term decisions— getting a degree, buying a house, starting a family—that's when they'd start to assess whether their employer could provide the ongoing supports they'd need, or whether they'd have to look elsewhere. So don't just toss out benefits here and there when you feel like it—write those benefits into a clearly outlined policy. That way your employees can feel safe and confident in choosing to build their lives where they stand.

1 moment to master

You may be thinking that you can't afford to offer a full benefit package, but whatever your company's size, there's always some way to adapt these supports to your budget. So this week, open your mind to the idea of expanding on what you offer your employees. Start by looking for programs that could help you support your people's health and wellness—like the federal Small Business Health Options marketplace. And think about this: how much could you save on turnover if you began offering a compelling reason to stay long term, like a modest tuition spending account, a retirement savings top-up program, or even special benefits for parents like free diapers or family days off?

You may not always be able to offer more pay than your competitors, but you can always find creative ways to provide your people with a better life. That's how you turn "how much longer can I stay here?" into "why would I ever leave?"

MANAGEMENT MASTERCLASS SELF-ASSESSMENT

Module Review:
Mastering Your Moments Video 3

SECTION 3

How to Earn "I Love It Here"

Part 1: Quiz

1. The root cause of 75% of turnover can be traced back to what single factor?

   a) Boredom

   b) Disagreements with co-workers

   c) Uncaring, inconsistent management

   d) Low pay/long hours

2. True or false: An employee retention specialist is responsible for hiring, payroll, conflict management, and benefit administration.

   ☐ True
   ☐ False

3. From the lessons in this section, what is one of the most loyalty-inspiring forms of value you can offer an employee beyond a higher wage?

   a) A high-status title

   b) Flex time

   c) A designated parking stall

   d) A desk by a window

4. List three of the seven ways to promote a culture of recognition that were outlined in this section.

   1. _____

   2. _____

   3. _____

5. What are the three signs of burnout?

   a) Tiredness, lateness, absences

   b) Negativity, procrastination, apathy

   c) Argumentativeness, shoddy work, missed deadlines

   d) Distracted behavior, web surfing, doodling in meetings

6. "At the end of the day, an organization is a simply a _____."

   a) Generator of wealth

   b) Form of hierarchy

   c) Metaphorical schoolyard

   d) Collection of people

7. List four of the ten ways to offer an employee recognition that were listed in this section.

1. _____

2. _____

3. _____

4. _____

Part 1: Answers

1. C: Uncaring, inconsistent management (see lesson 3.1)

2. False. This is role is about retention and engagement, not human resources (see lesson 3.2)

3. B: Flex time (see lesson 3.3)

4. Any of: Flex time, extra vacation, telecommuting, profit sharing/equity, vocal praise, flex work/vacation, free food, gifts/prizes, recognition programs, bonus money, experiences (see lesson 3.4)

5. B: Negativity, procrastination, apathy (see lesson 3.5)

6. D: Collection of people—as said by Freek Vermeulen (see lesson 3.6)

7. Any of: Healthcare plan, retirement savings, support for starting a family, tuition/education support, fitness support or gym membership, free food, staff discounts, stress busters, EAPs, free time (see lesson 3.7)

Part 2: "Mastering Your Moments" Checklist

By the end of this section, I have:

1. Considered the last time an employee quit, and, in retrospect, the signs that preceded that departure.

   GO DEEPER:

   ☐ If it was a surprise, why?

   ☐ Would you still be taken by surprise if the same chain of events were to occur today?

   ☐ What could you have done differently that might have created a better outcome?

2. Identified someone on my team who could have the potential to become an employee retention specialist.

GO DEEPER:

☐ What qualities made you choose that person?

☐ What tools, support, or training could you give them to grow into such a role?

_____

_____

_____

_____

_____

_____

_____

_____

_____

_____

_____

_____

3. Made a list of the employees who are adding the most value to my company, and considered ways to increase the value my company is offering them.

GO DEEPER:

☐ How are you defining value as you create this list?

☐ What employees are delivering critical value beyond the bottom line?

4. Created an opportunity to publicly praise each person on my team for the unique and specific contributions they have made over the past week or month.

GO DEEPER:

- [ ] Was this exercise difficult for you?
- [ ] If so, why? Was it simple shyness, or something else?
- [ ] What, if anything, changed on your team after you created this moment?

5. Analyzed the behavior of the people on my team for the three signs of burnout (negativity, procrastination, apathy).

GO DEEPER:

☐ Did you identify any at-risk individuals?

☐ What can you change to better empower, encourage, or communicate with them?

☐ If they can't or don't wish to re-engage, what will you do to help coach them into a better-fitting role?

6. Written down three adjectives to define my current workplace culture, along with three to describe my ideal workplace culture.

GO DEEPER:

☐ How different are your two lists?

☐ What one word on your "current" list would you most like to see change?

☐ What single adjective would you pick as your key goal to work toward?

7. Analyzed the full value of the benefits package I am offering my employees, and considered what non-salary benefits I could offer to improve retention.

GO DEEPER:

☐ How do you view the exchange of value between your company and your employees? Is it a partnership? Or do you see the relationship as unbalanced?

☐ Do you think your employees view the relationship the same way?

— 4 —

SPARKING THE POSSIBILITY

4.1

HOW TO BE REMEMBERED FOREVER

VIDEO 23

The radical power of recognizing potential

1 big idea

Servant leadership may seem like a commitment to humility, but don't let fears of self-erasure keep you off the path. The fact is, centering the needs of your employees over your own can be like writing your name in the sky.

2 insights from our workplace research

1. If you've ever heard me speak about my old teacher Mr. Jensen,[4] you'll know that I believe—more than believe, *know*—that a single moment in time can change a person's life. In our years of research, we've collected mountains of powerful stories from employees of all ages who can describe the exact moment a boss helped them truly envision what they could become in their career and in their life. A handwritten letter that thanked them for their contributions or acknowledged their growth and talent. A simple conversation or phone call where their boss told them about the future they could have at their company. Even a simple thing, like a nice review on LinkedIn or the gift of a personalized book—all of these actions have created a lasting impact, and cemented a mentor in someone's memory forever.

2. The best of these moments raise an employee up on two fronts: they communicate *worth*, and they communicate *potential*. That co-worker who everyone says is too chatty? Their ability to build relationships and set people at ease could be a superpower in the right environment. That junior staff member who chafes against authority? Give them total creative control over a single test project and see where that sense of independence can take them. Each of your employees needs to know that that when you look at them, you don't see a problem—you see a person with value.

1 moment to master

This week, find an opportunity to advocate for one of your employees by expressing to them what kind of talent and potential you can see in them. This isn't about trying to uncover some astonishing, never-before-seen greatness—if you pay attention to who they really are, you can do this for *any* of your employees, even the ones you might find difficult. (Especially the ones you might find difficult!) You're advocating for your people to become their best, but not by pushing them to be the best *in* the world. What you're doing is encouraging them to become the best *for* the world: you're helping them uncover their own brand of greatness so they can bring it to their work, family, and community every day.

Don't hold back, or reserve your praise for when they "deserve" it—write that note, have that conversation, and lift your employees up with your advocacy today. Offer your shoulders so they can see their potential, and your name will never die.

4.2

ARE YOU TRYING TO MAKE FIRE WITH NO FUEL?

VIDEO 24

How to turn potential into ability

1 big idea

You can't stand in front of a fireplace and say "give me heat, then I'll give you wood" and expect to get warm. Just like you can't expect results from your employees before you give them any tools to achieve them with.

2 insights from our workplace research

1. Potential is great, it's amazing—and your employees will love you for recognizing it. But if you try to cold-start them into more responsibility without first equipping them with lots of opportunities to grow into it, you're just trying to build a fire with no fuel. And when we talk to employees who face this situation, what we see is mistakes, frustration, and burnout.

2. As a Mentor Manager, it's your job to provide the kindling that can turn that spark of potential into the sustaining flame of ability. In our research, we've seen three types of "fuel" that can really kick off this type of development:

   Meaningful books
   Seriously! The gift of a carefully chosen business or career development book can galvanize an employee and create a cherished moment they'll remember forever.

Speakers and workshops

Expert lunch-and-learns, online courses, group webinars—you get the idea. Polling your team on what they want to learn can go even further in investing them in that training.

Your advocacy

This is critical: show them that you see their unique potential, and help them see it too. Always be on the lookout for opportunities to design moments of praise or development that are specific to each employee.

1 moment to master

Leadership skills like communication, motivation, trust, teamwork, conflict resolution, delegation, and creativity are the energy your people want to bring to the world. This week, I want you to try feeding that fire for just one person on your team.

Is there an employee with leadership potential who might be inspired by a book like *Good to Great*, *You Are a Badass*, or *Dare to Lead*? Is there a local or online conference on the horizon that might connect an employee more deeply with their industry? Or simply start by asking—say: "I see this in you, and I think we can make use of it. Is there a masterclass you would like to take?"

Start with one, and see where it goes. I bet you'll be inspired to keep igniting that spark across your whole team.

4.3

WHY HIRE FOR A JOB WHEN YOU COULD HIRE FOR A HERO?

How great leaders use story to
connect employees with their purpose

1 big idea

If it needs doing, it has *meaning*. Every job affects other people in some way, which means every job has purpose, and offers the opportunity to show up as a hero.

2 insights from our workplace research

1. The trick to connecting an employee with their purpose is to find the *story*. I once consulted with a school district in California that was having trouble keeping janitorial staff. (If you have kids, you can guess why: it's a tough, noisy, messy, chaotic job!) But one day, in one school, the principal did something different: she asked a few classes to write letters to the janitor to thank him for what he did every day. What an effect! One moment he sees his job as mopping floors, the next moment he sees himself through the kids' eyes: helping them stay safe, making them feel comfortable and welcome as they walk in every day, stopping to chat in the hall when they're feeling sad or lonely. So long floor-mopper, hello superman—and the best part is, that story is *true*.

2. The words you use to describe a job are a critical part of this story building—so long as they're authentic. Think of the difference between a construction worker and a home builder. One is hammering nails, the other is creating a refuge and a legacy for a family. But be careful: if your workplace culture is serious, don't use cutesy phrases like "dream weavers" or "assistance fairies." Name and speak about your roles in a way that is meaningful but truthful, using terms that your specific employees will feel proud to say.

1 moment to master

To design a better story for your employees, start with the value their jobs bring to the world—not just the *what*, but the *why*. This week, think about how each of the roles at your company might offer the opportunity to affect other people in a positive way. That greeter? She's giving each person a moment of human contact in a world that can feel alienating. That dental assistant? He's setting people at ease in a scary situation.

And one more thing: don't forget to also think about the way you talk about and define each job—and the people who are doing that work. Do you direct your customers to go speak to the "front desk" or to "Angela at reception"? In the context of your specific culture, do the titles you give your employees make them feel silly or inspired?

Using better words and telling a better story is not fake, it's *framing*—you're simply relating the same truth, but in a way that centers the person, not the position. That's how you turn a team of workers into a team of heroes.

4.4

GIVE YOUR EMPLOYEES THE WHEEL AND LET THEM DRIVE

4 ways to invest your team in your business

1 big idea

You know that moment when you're a kid and you get a first taste of control over something *big*? For me, it was when my dad sat me on his lap and let me take the wheel of the car for the very first time. It was a monumental shift in perspective that invested me *completely* in the act of driving, in a way being a passenger never did.

Want to see a total transformation in your workplace? Hand over the wheel and let your employees drive.

2 insights from our workplace research

1. Across all of our case studies, the feeling of control has been the biggest game changer in terms of getting a team of employees invested in the success of the business. Empowering your people with responsibility and authority builds trust, provides purpose, and opens the door for you to offer better mentorship. The key is to release that authority in small steps—remember: my dad didn't just plop me in the driver's seat and hand me the keys. He chose an empty street, kept his own feet on the pedals, and held his hands at the ready to correct our path if I strayed too far in our lane.

2. A great place to start is by giving your employees room to accomplish a project on their own terms—or even to give them more flexibility in how they execute their daily work. Set your standards, deadlines, and deliverables, then step back and let them come up with a plan to get it done, and done well. Guide them to resources they can use, let them know who they can or should collaborate with, and facilitate any connections that need to be made. From there, let them know your door is open, but they are free to get the work done when and how they see fit (with you keeping a subtle eye on their progress and stepping in when absolutely needed, of course).

The result? Employees who are invested in the *outcome*, not in the appearance of busywork.

1 moment to master

If you're not sure where to start, the best strategy is to ask. What does taking control look like to your employees? What do *they* want to take charge of? So, this week, hold a conversation with each of your employees to find out if there is a project they'd like to take charge of (or launch!), if they're interested in redesigning their work schedule, or if there is an extra responsibility or skill set they've been wanting to step into, such as being involved in hiring decisions. Then—and this is the kicker—task them with designing the plan to make it happen.

4.5
HOW TO LOVE EVERYONE

What it means to catch people doing good

1 big idea

Here's one of the world's great mysteries: If criticism wears people down and praise builds them up, why is it so *easy* as a leader to tell your people what they're doing wrong, but so *hard* to tell them about everything they get right?

2 insights from our workplace research

1. Praise requires confidence—both to give it, and to receive it with grace. But it's also one of the *foundations* of confidence. So by making the effort to send praise out into the world, you're actually amplifying that sense of confidence by building it up in your employees, and in yourself. In a sense, it's a way of freeing your employees to embrace the joy of being truly engaged in their work, and at the same time freeing yourself to feel genuine love for the people you lead and serve.

2. We've learned from great leaders that the most effective way to offer praise is to *catch people doing good*, right at the moment when they're doing it. When you see an employee making a positive difference—lending an extra hand to a customer who needs it, stepping in with a clever solution to some everyday hiccup—don't hold back! Show them you that see the value they bring, even if they didn't realize they were bringing value in that moment. As one leader told me, by helping people recognize the value they bring, even in their smallest actions, you can help them embrace their own ability to contribute to the world.

1 moment to master

If you're not used to offering praise, it can feel uncomfortable at first. So this week, give yourself a head start by doing a little preparation. Write down the names of every employee you manage, and, for each, list three things that person excels at, whether that's a specific skill or task, or even just something about their personality or the way they interact with others.

Now you're in a great position to create a moment for every one of the people on your list. Find an opportunity for each employee to praise them for one of their strengths—intentionally, directly, and out loud. Catch them in the act if you can, but even if that perfect opportunity doesn't arise, make the effort anyway. Start a conversation, call them out in a meeting, or even make a special phone call.

So few managers take the time, but this kind of vocal praise really, really matters to your staff. You'll be helping each one of your people recognize what a difference they can make when they bring their best selves to work every day.

4.6

THIS STRATEGY IS KILLING YOUR BUSINESS

VIDEO 28

The 3 questions you need to ask your employees right now

1 big idea

The exit interview is one of the most baffling management tools we come across in our workplace research. Why wait until an employee's last day on the job to ask them what would have made them happy? That's like a hospital keeping its heart monitor in the morgue.

2 insights from our workplace research

1. Great leaders we've worked with continually check the vitals of their employees all the time, not just when they show signs of disengagement. They do it by holding regular status interviews with each individual—not to critique their performance, but to take an accurate measure of what that employee is feeling and what resources and support they might need to be able to perform at their best.

2. Status interviews are most effective when are conscientiously planned yet feel spontaneous. You want to ask very specific questions that will help you plan a route forward together, like:

   - "What can we do to keep you here?"

   - "What's getting in the way of you reaching your maximum success?"

   - "How can I help you get where you want to go?"

But by ditching formality and instead finding an "unplanned" moment where you can hold this conversation more casually, you avoid making the employee feel like just another task you're checking off your list—giving you a better chance at an authentic interaction that results in genuine connection and insight.

1 moment to master

This week, have a look at your calendar for the month ahead and schedule a moment for a status interview with each employee. Don't pounce, but be casual: simply call them aside, and ask the questions that will help uncover that employee's current needs and interests. And, hey, why not take the opportunity to acknowledge their contributions and offer a bit of vocal praise while you're at it.

But don't stop there! The important part is to make a plan. After you've held an interview, decide on a next step for that employee, one that will move them a bit closer to their personal or professional ambitions—and do this for *each person*, even if it seems like everything is fine with some individuals. Because an employee's last day on the job is the wrong time to find out what might have helped them to love working for your company.

4.7
HAVE YOU GROUNDED YOUR EMPLOYEES?

VIDEO 29

The 4 elements of a growth development plan

1 big idea

The leaders we meet who truly make an impact never say "stay grounded" when an employee comes to them with a sky-high dream. They say: "Hey, that's amazing. Now let's build you a plane so you can reach that cloud."

2 insights from our workplace research

1. In aviation we always say, "Airplanes don't get lost, pilots do." That's why you never take off without creating a flight plan: direction, destination, frequencies, weather, markers, and any diversion that might crop up along the way. As you've been working through this Management Masterclass Series, I hope you've started checking in regularly with your employees to assess their status and learn their goals. But if you want each of your people to actually *achieve* those goals, they need a flight plan too—or, in this case, a growth development plan.

2. Just like a flight plan, a growth development plan should be simple, realistic, and associated with time. Take that big dream and work with your employee to map out the specific, outcome-oriented, and scheduled actions that will get them to their destination.

   Start with small, achievable steps, and work in accountability and deadlines for the actions each of you will take—and that "each" is important, because you're integral to this plan too. Let's say they want to get their MBA. Step one for the employee might be to take a night course to meet a pre-requisite. Step one for you might be to draft a plan for delegating some of their workload while they're doing the program.

1 moment to master

This week, think of one employee who has expressed a clear goal—maybe during a status interview, maybe just in conversation. Now, map it out: If that's their destination, what does the sky look like between here and there? Where are the layovers? What kind of turbulence should you both prepare for?

Once you've envisioned the route, schedule a new meeting with that employee so you can hash out what each of you is willing to do to start moving forward. From there, it's up to your employee to decide if they want that dream badly enough to follow through. Either way, simply by making the effort to show them a route map instead of a red flag, you'll have created a moment of mentorship they'll remember forever.

4.8

ARE YOU PROMOTING A BUDDY OR A BOSS?

VIDEO 30

How to help an employee into leadership

1 big idea

So you've got this person on your team who's easy to talk to, makes the workday feel fun, and everybody just seems to get along with them. Sounds like leadership potential, right?

But hold on—before you throw them into management, take a closer look. Are you promoting someone who can be the boss? Or are you just promoting everyone's buddy?

2 insights from our workplace research

1. We see it happen all the time. A leader wants to promote from within (check, excellent idea), examines their staff for talent (double check, doing great so far), and then lands on that person who's a friend to everyone. So they put them in charge of all those co-workers who seem to like them so much and—record scratch—it just doesn't work. Suddenly the team pushes back and won't take orders, or your new manager isn't even giving any direction at all.

   If you've read my book you'll be familiar with the four types of managers, and you might even recognize who we're talking about here. Meet the Buddy Manager, who achieves a high level of friendship and connection with everyone on their team, but maintains almost no standards or expectations at all. The end result in your workforce? Complacency, entitlement, resentment, and a lack of professional growth.

2. To avoid promoting a Buddy Manager—or to recognize when you need to mentor a budding buddy into someone who can lead—make sure that your management candidate is *respected* more than they are liked. Do they uphold high standards for themselves and their team? Are they able to inspire and rally their co-workers to follow that example? And are they *already* taking a mentorship role, even if they're not yet in a position of authority?

1 moment to master

Everyone has a few "buddies" on their team, and being a friend to everyone isn't necessarily a dealbreaker when it comes time to promote from within. But it *does* mean that candidate needs more advocacy and development from you, to help them see what they could become if they would step up into caring authority.

So this week, take a look at a few of the buddies in your workplace and think about who might show leadership potential with a little time and guidance. If they learned to take charge, could they lead their existing team, or would it be better for them to start fresh in a new department? What resources and training could you give them to help them become more aware of their effect on their team? Take it slow, but do put in the effort—because there's nothing quite like the feeling of watching a buddy grow into being a boss.

MANAGEMENT MASTERCLASS SELF-ASSESSMENT

Module Review:
Mastering Your Moments Video 4

SECTION 4

Sparking the Possibility

Part 1: Quiz

1. List three of the impactful actions you learned about in this section that could help an employee recognize their own potential.

   1. _____

   2. _____

   3. _____

2. If you want to help an employee turn talent into ability, you have to offer "fuel" in the form of:

   a) Honest critique

   b) Lots of oversight and profound advice

   c) Repeated barriers to learn to overcome

   d) Opportunities for growth

3. You can connect your employees more deeply with their job's greater purpose by using elements of:

a) Philosophy

b) Storytelling

c) Military strategy

d) Architectural theory

4. What are two of the four top ways to "hand over the wheel" and invest your employees in the success of your organization?

1. _____

2. _____

5. What does it mean to "catch people doing good"?

a) Always be observing your employees

b) Make charity work mandatory at your company

c) Find lots of opportunities to offer vocal praise

d) Ask new hires about their volunteer experiences

6. True or false: Growth development plans work best when your employees create them on their own.

☐ True

☐ False

7. A three-question "status interview" is:

a) An informal but structured conversation that you do not need to schedule

b) A way to help you determine an employee's raise at their annual review

c) An important part of the exit process to help you learn why an employee quit

d) A collective voting process to collect staff feedback

8. What is the most important quality to look for when promoting from within your team?

a) Someone who everyone on the team thinks of as a good buddy

b) Someone who is good at getting people to do things

c) Someone who is very ambitious

d) Someone who the team looks to for mentorship

Part 1: Answers

1. Any of: Offer a personalized gift reflects their talent, write a handwritten letter, call them on the phone to offer praise, review them on LinkedIn, express your admiration to their family (see lesson 4.1)

2. D: Opportunities for growth (see lesson 4.2)

3. B: Storytelling (see lesson 4.3)

4. Any of: Involve them in hiring decisions, allow for flexible schedules, ask for ideas, delegate responsibility (see lesson 4.4)

5. C: Find lots of opportunities to offer vocal praise (see lesson 4.5)

6. False: Growth development plans are best developed and carried out by a manager and an employee in partnership (see lesson 4.7)

7. A: An informal but structured conversation that you do not need to schedule (see lesson 4.6)

8. D: Someone who the team looks to for mentorship (see lesson 4.8)

Part 2: "Mastering Your Moments" Checklist

By the end of this section, I have:

1. Made a list of all my direct employees, and named three unique strengths for each individual.

   GO DEEPER:

   ☐ How often do you communicate these strengths to each employee?

   ☐ If not often, what is it that's holding you back?

2. Created an individual moment for an employee that could help them see their unique talent and potential.

GO DEEPER:

☐ What kind of reaction did you receive?

☐ How did it change their relationship with their work?

☐ Can you design a similar moment for each one of your employees?

3. Created a growth opportunity for an employee that is specific to their talents, interests, or leadership goals.

GO DEEPER:

☐ What led you to choose the specific growth opportunity you offered (e.g., book, seminar, other form of advocacy)?

☐ What was the immediate result?

4. Made a list of the positions and roles under my leadership, and defined the single purpose or "why" of that role that makes it meaningful.

GO DEEPER:

☐ Will the story you are telling about each role feel authentic to the people who perform it?

☐ If the story resonates as genuine, how can you weave it further through the title, terminology, and description of duties?

5. Taken steps to "hand over the wheel" to my employees and given them more control and autonomy in the way they do their work.

GO DEEPER:

☐ If you find it hard to give your employees more control, what is at the root of that lack of trust?

☐ What could you gain by learning to step back more often?

☐ If you don't trust your employees to accomplish their work effectively, what should you change about your hiring or training processes?

6. Assessed the members of my team for leadership potential and/or ambition.

GO DEEPER:

☐ If an employee has obvious mentorship abilities, what will you do to show them they have leadership opportunities within your company?

☐ If a potential leader has close friendships on their current team that could cause friction if the leadership dynamics are changed, what opportunities exist in a different team or department?

7. Scheduled a time in the near future for a status interview with each of my direct employees.

GO DEEPER:

☐ Have you been surprised by the answers you are receiving to the three key status interview questions?

☐ As you hold these interviews, what are you realizing about your work culture that you did not see before?

8. Began working with each employee to create a growth development plan.

GO DEEPER:

☐ Are you making sure to include a list of concrete milestones for both the employee and yourself in each plan?

☐ What role have your status interviews been playing as you and your employees envision and develop their goals and milestones?

— 5 —

ALWAYS BE FLYING THE AIRPLANE

THE DEF LEPPARD EFFECT

Developing vs. advocating—and why you need both

1 big idea

When I was twelve, I asked my mother for a drum kit, and she told me that when I got my then-middling grades up to As and Bs, I could have it. That standard-setting was a form of development, and it helped me get where I needed to be.

My father, meanwhile, overheard and called me over to his CD shelf. He pulled out a couple of Rush albums and told me to listen carefully to the incredible Neil Peart. Then he pulled out *Hysteria* by Def Leppard and described how Rick Allen made it big despite having only one arm. I listened to those albums and imagined it: pictured those drummers on stage; pictured *me*, playing at that level.

That was advocacy. And you owe your employees both.

2 insights from our workplace research

1. Many of the companies we research have great development programs: well-worn career paths that employees can move through to reach more responsibility or better pay. But advocating is different from development: it's not just skill-building, it's the art of revealing hidden potential—each employee's *specific, individual* potential. That's what sparks someone to truly connect with a goal, and to get fired up to pursue it.

2. This is not either/or. Once you lift an employee up to show them where the road can take them, you have to give them the individual tools they need to develop those skills and abilities. Corporate

career paths are great, but the best leaders we've met don't default to those. Think personal: What's the next step for *this* employee if they want to follow *that* career path? What achievements do they need? What expectations can you set to drive them toward those achievements?

1 moment to master

This week, start adding some advocacy to the development you already offer your people (at least that I hope you offer!). Make a list each of each employee and name 1) the skill they most excel at, and 2) an exciting career goal that would best utilize that skill. Is it executive leadership? Elite sales? Directing major projects? Choose something aspirational, and suited just to them.

Next, schedule time over the weeks ahead to have a conversation with each person on your list in which you communicate where you can imagine them going, and what specific value they would bring to that role. Pair that inspiration with a development plan to get there, and you've put the whole picture in place: from drum kit to concert hall.

5.2

COMPASSION OR YOUR DEADLINE— DOES A LEADER HAVE TO CHOOSE?

VIDEO 32

How to help an employee through a crisis (and still get the work done)

1 big idea

When someone on your team is in the middle of a crisis, sometimes it's all you can see—you get nervous; you waver between hovering and avoidance; you might even feel guilty for worrying about the work.

But here's something to remember that can help you push past that awkwardness: your employee is *more* than their crisis.

2 insights from our workplace research

1. As much as you might wish those thoughts away, it's natural to have secret worries about errors or schedules when someone on your team is struggling with an awful event. But when employees tell us about the bosses who earned their loyalty in tough times, they talk about the ones who arrive with compassion *first*.

    How can you manage that when all you feel is stress? You keep things separate. To your employee, you show care, support, and a listening ear. When you're with your peers, that's the time to unload all those concerns about deadlines and dropped balls.

2. The best managers we've met always saw each of their employees as a whole person—especially during a crisis. Whatever they're going through, make sure it isn't the subject of every conversation you have. If you used to talk about sports or kids or movies, keep doing that. If work is helping them hold it together, follow their lead and discuss the work, just like before. Treating an employee in crisis like they're still who they always were can help them feel more like themselves too.

1 moment to master

A great way to stay on track when someone on your team gets side-swiped is to have a plan at the ready. This week, take some time to review the supports your company offers, like paid time off, counselling, loans, or an EAP. Then, get familiar with the terms and what an employee would need to do to access those benefits.

Don't forget to assess your team's readiness to act as a support network too: Do you have a phone tree or chat group that could quickly raise a meal-delivery or fundraising army? Who could you call on to step in or take on extra duties if needed? (Though keep privacy in mind: always get permission from the employee before revealing any personal information.) Sketching out what your team can do before a crisis hits can help you avoid brainlock later, when emotions are high.

5.3

ALWAYS BE FLYING
THE AIRPLANE

VIDEO 33

The problem with piloting by personality type

1 big idea

The most important lesson about leading humans I ever received happened in the cockpit of a plane when I was a teen in flight school. And it's this: *Always be flying the airplane.*

Here's the kicker, though: you can't just fly the machine you read about in the training manual. You have to fly the airplane you're actually in.

2 insights from our workplace research

1. Even if they're the same model and came off the same manufacturing line, no two individual planes will ever fly exactly alike. And the same is true with people. However popular systems like the Enneagram or Hartman Color Code have become in leadership circles, a personality test will never be able to tell you how a particular individual truly needs to be managed. That's the real danger we see when managers rely too much on personality types to try to understand their people: once you put someone in a box and decide that you know who they are, you tend to *keep* them in that box.

   And then? You're not leading the person anymore. You're leading the box.

2. In researching mentor management, I've come to understand that it requires the same commitment to rejecting assumptions that I learned on those planes. In flight school, we had to always stay in tune with the craft we were flying: checking instruments, evaluating, adjusting...on repeat and repeat and repeat. Effective leaders do the same with their employees: observing and connecting to learn more about who they are, what they're best at, how they're doing in the moment, and what gives them purpose.

Just like with an airplane, there are no shortcuts—you have to be constantly checking their status, evaluating their needs, and determining the next action that will help them reach their goals. And you have to continue doing this for as long as that employee is under your leadership.

1 moment to master

This week, test out your assumptions by taking a fresh look at one person under your leadership. Think about an employee you've been having difficulty with, or who doesn't seem to connect with their work. When you call that person to mind, what preconceptions come up about who they are, or how they might react to a given situation? What cycles keep repeating that have been frustrating you, or them?

Now, put away your ideas about how you think they need to be led, and look at that employee through a new lens—as an individual. What one thing about your management style could you tweak or customize to see if you can relate to them in a new way? Think small actions: perhaps a little more empathy, a bit of extra praise, some positive guidance instead of criticism.

Pay attention to how they respond to your changes, and adjust as needed—just like you're flying an airplane. Because personality tests can be an interesting experiment, but if you want to truly understand someone, nothing can replace authentic, individual connection.

5.4

THE ONLY BAD WORD
IN MANAGEMENT

VIDEO 34

What mangers MUST do when they start feeling callous

1 big idea

Real talk time: Did you become a leader because you love mentoring people, or is managing others something you tolerate as a necessary step up the corporate ladder?

If it's the second thing, consider this: management isn't actually a promotion if you hate it.

2 insights from our workplace research

1. Sometimes in our research, we meet a leader who is just done. They can't connect. They avoid their employees, or at best go through the motions. They've hit that one wall in management you never want to hit: they've become callous.

    If this feels familiar, you're not alone and you don't need to feel guilty. But you *do* need to look inside and uncover what's driving that weariness, so you know what kind of change you need to make. You were probably promoted because you were great at your job— but there are lots of ways to bring value to an organization, and lots of ways to move forward in a career. Maybe you're creative, a technical wiz, a problem solver, even a rainmaker... all great qualities deserving of promotion, but not necessarily into the management of people. For that role, you need stewardship, empathy, caring, and the ability to motivate and inspire.

2. If being a mentor has brought you joy but you're feeling disconnected anyway, you still need to make a change. Consult with your peers, your boss, or your own circle of mentors to get some outside perspective on what's creating that gap, and ask for help in reconnecting with that part of you that cares. It may be as simple as taking some time off, or you may need to take larger steps to shake up a tired routine. We've seen great results from a burned-out manager launching a daily mindfulness practice, taking a leadership course to refresh how they relate to people, or even moving to a new department to get away from some dug-in dynamics.

1 moment to master

This week, it's time to get introspective. Ask yourself one question: *Does leadership make me happy?*

At heart, beyond any feelings of exhaustion or burnout, are you interested in the dreams, talents, and hobbies of the people you manage? When they come to you with complaints or worries, do you want to listen? Are you willing to put the spotlight on *them* so *they* can shine?

If your answer is yes, great—you may need to work on your time or stress management, but you're on the right path. And if it's no? That's okay too. Really, it's okay! But now it's time to be brave and start looking for a role that does light you up—because you deserve to be happy. Think back to the last position where the work resonated with you, whether that was sales, creative thinking, project development, or something more technical. Then examine the opportunities in those career tracks and start building a new path of growth and seniority there.

5.5

DO YOU KNOW WHAT YOUR TEAM IS REALLY SAYING?

VIDEO 35

How not to get blindsided by negative employee feedback

1 big idea

If you've got that "manager" label on your shirt, your people most definitely have opinions about the way you lead. The problem is that they're rarely going to say it to your face.

2 insights from our workplace research

1. There is so little incentive and so much cost for any employee to tell their boss the honest truth about how they are being managed. That's why most leaders we meet have no idea that *they* are the root cause of problems in their workplace.

   But what we've learned from managers who've bridged that gap is that it is possible to hear and accept a need for change without letting it undermine your confidence. Step one is to state that you make mistakes—out loud, directly to your employees—and to announce that you are open to feedback, even if it's difficult. Step two is to genuinely welcome that feedback, and to actually *thank* your employees for their criticism when they offer it.

2. Sometimes emotion takes over and it's too hard to accept critical feedback for the gift that it is. When that happens, walk away. Take the time you need to calm down, and to weigh what you've

heard against the standards you've set for yourself as a mentor. But always remember that, even if it doesn't match your reality, your employee is telling their truth. It matters a lot to them, so set your ego aside and make it matter to you, too.

1 moment to master

They say management can be lonely, but it doesn't have to be that way. This week, analyze your professional and social networks and think about who among your peers has the right ingredients to offer some clear-eyed perspective when you are faced with difficult feedback—ingredients like experience, empathy, discretion, and a shared commitment to the principles of mentorship. It could be a friend, a colleague, perhaps even your own boss—basically, someone you trust who has likely faced similar problems.

Then, when you do hear something uncomfortable that you're not sure is fair, open yourself up to that peer and say, "I've had this situation and I don't know what to think." Their outside view can help you understand that, as a leader, you're simply subject to scrutiny—it's part of the role.

5.6

THE THUMBTACK PRINCIPLE

How to show your employees that you support their dreams

1 big idea

If you've ever taken a course on writing, you'll know the phrase "show, don't tell." Well, the same idea applies to management: it's one thing to *say* something is true, but it's another thing altogether to prove that truth to your employees.

2 insights from our workplace research

1. One of the best examples of caring leadership my team and I have witnessed was during our research into a successful chain of tire stores. The manager of one store, Frank, had achieved a retention rate that blew the rest of his industry out of the water—his employees had an average of ten years on the job, and the whole team had obvious and deep camaraderie. So I asked Frank his secret, and he said: "These are my people. What matters to them matters to me." More importantly, he actually *demonstrated* that priority by taking action to help his people get the things that mattered to them.

2. Here's the best part: the staff at that tire store knew their dreams meant something to Frank because they could literally see it. When Frank learned about a team member's vision for their future— buying a boat, a down payment on a house, starting a family, going back to school—he would print out a picture to represent that vision, then pin it up on the wall of his office with a thumbtack.

Every day, each employee at that store could see their own biggest dream, along with everybody else's. That reminded everyone that they were all working toward each other's goals as a team.

1 moment to master

This week's challenge is for the leaders who have already built a foundation of open communication with their team. (Not there yet? It's time to go back to the basics!) What extra step could you be taking to demonstrate to your employees that their goals and dreams matter to you? Think about ways you could represent those dreams in a physical or visual way in your workplace—whether that's a thumbtack collage like Frank's, or something more suited to your unique office culture.

Once you've done that, go one step further and meet with each employee to create a plan to start moving them toward their vision. How many extra hours would they need to work to reach that down payment? What kind of a milestone would earn that extra vacation week? What new training could prepare them to move into that coveted role? The road map you create together can change those 2-D thumbtacked pictures into their real-world life—and earn you a place in their memory forever.

5.7

DANGER ALERT!
BRACE FOR IMPACT!

VIDEO 37

What COVID-19 taught us about managing through a disaster

1 big idea

When a crisis hits, your employees don't have to be just one more part of the problem you need to solve. They're actually a big part of the *solution*—if, that is, you can invest them in finding a way out together.

2 insights from our workplace research

1. The pandemic taught our research team a lot about how effective leaders rally their teams through daunting upheaval and economic hardship. The first lesson? *Stay flexible.* If you want to survive macro-level change—whether that's industry disruption, a takeover, a downturn, a society-shuttering virus, or the next curveball the world is going to throw at us—you have to be prepared to adapt, a lot.

    Remember how the rules kept changing during COVID? The companies that survived were the ones that didn't get hung up on one way of doing things: new safety protocols, more hours, fewer hours, Zoom meetings, selling product out the window, whatever it took. They also tapped their employees for great ideas, whether that was ways of collaborating digitally, new potential revenue streams, or maintaining relationships with customers and supporters while their doors were closed.

2. The best recoveries we've seen from any kind of crisis came out of an open leadership culture. If you don't want the rumor mill to control the story, tell your people what's going on: the problem you're facing, how you're addressing it, and what they can expect from you. Yes, be positive and show them the hope, but stick to the *truth*: if there are risks or challenges ahead, like payroll cutbacks or longer days, don't promise otherwise. If you've been investing in building trust, your people are likely to stay by you—and work with you to push through that rough patch. But if they find out you've been manipulating them, they'll walk.

Most importantly, be prepared to share in any sacrifices you ask for. This is your opportunity to show your people what you stand for—when you're on the other side, they'll remember.

1 moment to master

This week, think back to the last big disaster that affected your business—whether that was COVID or something more local. How did you handle the sudden changes and setbacks, and how did your employees react? If something similar (or similarly unique) happened again, would you be more prepared? What would you change in how you communicated or collaborated with your employees?

There's never going to be a "last" crisis—unexpected events are always around the corner. But if you can use the lessons they teach to build trust with your team and create a better plan for next time, then at least that disaster didn't happen for nothing.

5.8
IS IT TIME FOR A HARD TALK?

How to hold a crucial conversation with your employee

1 big idea

Employees mess up sometimes (just like everyone), and once in a while you're going to have to face those hard talks. But before you get that conversation started, there's one extra step you need to take. You have to ask their permission.

2 insights from our workplace research

1. This comes straight from the employees we've interviewed: an unsolicited lecture, more often than not, is just going to trigger a person's defenses, leaving you feeling like you're shouting at a closed door. But by starting off with a simple statement—like "are you open to some feedback?"—you knock on that door, allowing your employee to *choose to open it*.

2. Once you have your employee's permission to have that difficult conversation, you are in the position to take on the role of advocate instead of critic. What you want is for your employee to understand that you're not there to defend the interests of the job, you're there to defend *them*, because—and here's the kicker—seeing them succeed at their job is important to you both.

We've seen that once an employee understands that you are there to advocate for their best interests, they become much more open to a conversation about the standards and expectations they need to meet, and what steps you'll need to take together to help them get there.

1 moment to master

This week, try practicing the art of asking permission to hold a difficult conversation—either with a trusted friend or colleague, or even in the mirror. Make sure your hypothetical request includes what needs to be addressed (i.e., the standards that aren't being met), an assurance that the conversation is safe and you are on their side (i.e., your advocacy), and an invitation that they can accept on their own terms.

Want a practice script? Here's one you can personalize to your own situation:

Hey Linda, your numbers have been down for the past three months. I don't know what's going on, but we have to find a way to turn it around. I want to check in and see how you're doing, and how I can help you set some goals and get back on track. Are you open to talking about this?

Permission, standards, advocacy, safety: these ingredients will result in a conversation that benefits you both. Include them all, stay calm, and keep your care for your employee front and center. The result will be a hard conversation that goes a lot easier for everyone.

5.9

BREAK IT UP!

VIDEO 39

Strategies for staying cool in a conflict

1 big idea

When your employees are fighting among each other, you can't let that chaotic energy wind you up. No matter how much anger, fear, or defensiveness surrounds you, it's your job as a manager to always have the lowest heart rate in the room.

2 insights from our workplace research

1. Workplace after workplace, we've seen that the vibe of every team flows directly from the leader. When they're aggressive, you need to be calm. When they're defensive, you need to be open. And when their minds are jumping from resentment about the past to fear about the future, you need to remain here, in the present. If you want things to stay cool, *you* have to stay cool. So rather than feeding off those high emotions, bring down your energy so you can help your people bring down theirs.

2. While you can and should set the tone for a calm and positive culture, keep in mind that you can't control other people. Leaders we've met who tried to police their employees' every thought and interaction just ended up driving that conflict underground rather than solving it. Your job is to create an environment in which people can manage themselves—and you do that by setting expectations for your employees and then offering them the support they need to reach them.

Treat your employees like moody children who can't get along, and that's likely how they'll act. So try treating your people like adults who can manage their own responsibilities and relationships. More often than not, they'll live up to that standard.

1 moment to master

This week, think about the last time there was a blow-up on your team, and how you reacted to that conflict. Did you blow up too, or were you able to keep your cool and bring everyone's temperature down a few degrees?

If you realize you've been letting other people wind you up instead of using your calm to wind them down, consider taking up a meditative practice, and dedicating a few minutes to it every day. Making that daily effort to center yourself will build the emotional muscle you need to maintain that lower heart rate when things get unsettled at work.

MANAGEMENT MASTERCLASS SELF-ASSESSMENT

Module Review:
Mastering Your Moments Video 5

SECTION 5

Always Be Flying the Airplane

Part 1: Quiz

1. If "developing" is about giving your employees lots of opportunity for growth, then "advocating" is about:

   a) Offering them a promotion

   b) Encouraging them to go back to school

   c) Encouraging them to see and reach for possibilities

   d) Protecting them from outside criticism

2. What order of steps you should take when an employee is hit with a personal crisis?

   a) Ensure deadlines are protected, re-work your schedules, ask if they need help

   b) Alert senior management, contact HR, place employment ad

   c) Ask if they need help, listen, give them space

   d) Listen, connect them with resources and support, rearrange your schedules

3. True or false: It is important to ask permission before entering a difficult or critical conversation with an employee.

☐ True

☐ False

4. Which of these words best defines the quality that is most harmful to a manager's ability to mentor others?

a) Weakness

b) Callousness

c) Laziness

d) Perfectionism

5. When an employee criticizes you, you should:

a) Thank them

b) Fire them

c) Admire them

d) Ignore them

6. What is the "Thumbtack Principle"?

a) A visual reminder for keeping your personal goals in sight

b) A visual reminder for keeping your employees' goals in sight

c) A KonMari inspired visual reminder for de-cluttering your office

d) A visual reminder for staying sharp

7. The companies that can successfully navigate economy-wide crises like the COVID-19 pandemic are the ones that:

a) Move fast and break things

b) Keep everything normal for employees for as long as possible

c) Ask for charity from their customers

d) Are prepared to adapt, and keep adapting

8. True or false: The Enneagram personality test is an almost infallible way to anticipate and manage employee behaviors.

☐ True

☐ False

9. When an employee loses their temper, the best response is to:

a) Tell them to go home and cool off

b) Match their energy to assert your authority

c) Keep your cool, and calmly repeat what they say to you in your own words

d) Walk away until everyone has calmed down

Part 1: Answers

1. C: Encouraging them to see and reach for possibilities (see lesson 5.1)

2. D: Listen, connect them with resources and support, rearrange your schedules (see lesson 5.2)

3. True: Asking for permission allows the employee to become a partner in the conversation, instead of a defensive victim of it (see lesson 5.8)

4. B: Callousness (see lesson 5.4)

5. A: Thank them (see lesson 5.5)

6. B: A visual reminder for keeping your employees' goals in sight (see lesson 5.6)

7. D: Are prepared to adapt, and keep adapting (see lesson 5.7)

8. False: Approaching any individual with a fixed or pre-determined idea of who they are can lead to misunderstandings (see lesson 5.3)

9. C: Keep your cool, and calmly repeat what they say to you in your own words (see lesson 5.9)

Part 2: "Mastering Your Moments" Checklist

By the end of this section, I have:

1. Made a list of a potential career goal for each of my employees that would be a great fit for their unique talents and goals—and communicated that possibility to each employee.

    GO DEEPER:

    ☐ Did these conversations spark new ideas or ambitions for any of your employees?

    ☐ What could you do now to help them move closer to that possibility?

2. Reviewed the support systems that my company could offer any employee who is hit with a personal crisis.

GO DEEPER:

☐ What would your first response to an employee's personal crisis be: To step back and give them space, or to take action and help?

☐ What are you worried could happen if you offered resources?

☐ How prepared are you to empathetically manage a crisis on your team in terms of scheduling, deliverables, and flexibility?

3. Identified an employee who I often have difficulty with, and conducted an "airplane experiment" by changing one thing in the way I communicate with or manage them.

GO DEEPER:

☐ What was the result of your experiment? Did anything change in your relationship or dynamic?

☐ How has this experiment changed the way you view that person?

☐ How has it changed the way they interact with you?

4. Considered the last few times an employee has come to me with an issue, and how I reacted to that interruption or request.

GO DEEPER:

☐ Was your initial instinct to lean in and engage? Or was is to internally roll your eyes?

☐ If you are starting to feel callous, how is that affecting your employees and their ability to thrive in your organization?

5. Considered how open I am to receiving criticism, and whether I have created a strong enough culture of trust to allow my employees to speak openly.

GO DEEPER:

☐ How did you react the last time an employee offered you criticism or challenging feedback? Are they likely to do it again?

☐ If you rarely or never receive criticism or challenging feedback, why do you think that is?

6. Asked each employee about their personal goals, and placed a visual reminder of those goals in my workspace.

GO DEEPER:

- [ ] How many of your employees had clear goals? What could you offer to help those who didn't to envision a possible ideal future?
- [ ] Were any of the goals different from what you thought they would be?
- [ ] What could you do right now to help each employee take a small step toward their goal?

7. Reviewed my (current or past) organization's response to the COVID-19 pandemic, and made a list of things we could change now to be better positioned to navigate the next unexpected crisis.

GO DEEPER:

☐ How much time do you spend on evaluation during and after each crisis you face?

☐ Have you ever repeated past mistakes when responding to a similar event? What could you do to avoid repeating such mistakes in the future?

8. Practiced ways to initiate a difficult or critical conversation that includes the four key elements of permission, standards, advocacy, and safety.

GO DEEPER:

☐ Are you likely to procrastinate or even avoid speaking openly with an employee who is not meeting your standards and expectations?

☐ If so, what has been the result of that avoidance? How could the employee have benefited from your honest advocacy?

9. Experimented with various meditative practices to help me keep my calm when confronted with conflict or anger.

GO DEEPER:

☐ How likely are you to keep your cool and have "the lowest heart rate in the room" in a conflict?

☐ What role do you typically play in the dynamics of office conflict?

☐ How often does anger or conflict get amplified by your reactions—or arise from you in the first place?

— **6** —

KEEPING THE MAIN THING THE MAIN THING

6.1
THE 3-BY-5
NOTECARD TEST

VIDEO 40

How to keep the main thing the main thing for you and your people

1 big idea

Simplicity is how you keep *the main thing the main thing*. If everyone who works for your business knows what direction they need to be facing, then all you have to do is keep walking.

2 insights from our workplace research

1. Of all of the practices we've seen implemented by exceptional leaders, the best has been a consistent effort to keep it simple. And I mean in *everything*: their business model, their schedule, the meetings they run, and the responsibilities they assign—right down to their personal lives. Trying to load too many choices, voices, tasks, and goals into every moment splits your attention and leaves everyone scattered and harried. As the leader, it's up to you to embody a workplace culture that has clarity, focus, space, and direction.

2. The foundation of a culture of simplicity lies in your messaging. If you were to ask everyone on your team to write out the mission of your company in one sentence, would they be able to do to it? Would you? Before you answer, consider this: when we do this test at the companies we research, a full 87% of employees are not able to give the right answer! It turns out that the vast majority of people have no idea which direction their company is facing—or which way they're facing within it.

If your company's vision statement isn't *brief, memorable,* and *authentic* to who you are and what you are trying to accomplish, then your employees do not have a goal they can move toward together. But a vision statement that does meet those three principles will give everyone on your team a clear, common direction for how they communicate, accomplish their tasks, and treat your customers.

1 moment to master

This week's challenge is to do the "3-by-5 test." Get a pack of 3-by-5-inch index cards, take one out, and—without looking anything up!—write down your organization's mission statement. Can you do it from memory? Is what you wrote accurate when you compare it to the official version? And even if it is, do those words feel truthful to what you're working on and how you're working at it?

Now, hand out the rest of those cards to the people on your team and ask them to try the same thing—not to test *them*, but to test the clarity, simplicity, and authenticity of your vision statement. If the results show that you aren't all facing in the same direction, it's time to rethink your messaging. Do the work to uncover what it is you're really trying to accomplish, and craft something new that's brief, memorable, and authentic—a few strong and true words that your people will feel proud to be associated with. That's going to help you all keep the main thing the main thing.

6.2
DON'T BE AFRAID
OF YOUR PHONE

VIDEO 41

Utilizing verbal communication instead
of hiding behind digital channels

1 big idea

Do you ever find yourself just a little bit exhausted after a day spent
using digital tools like Zoom and Slack? Sure, these innovations were
an absolute lifeline during the pandemic—but they've also led a lot of
us to forget a technology that's been a superstar at building connection for well over a century: the good ol' telephone.

2 insights from our workplace research

1. There are three very good reasons to consider picking up your
    phone before sending that text or that Zoom invite:

    - Holding that phone to your ear focuses your attention on the
      person you're speaking with, instead of on your web browser,
      your other text threads, or even that video inset of yourself.

    - The intimacy created by tone of voice, pauses, inflections,
      and genuine laughter (as opposed to "lols" or ☺) allows for
      better connection and mutual understanding.

    - And, finally, a phone conversation is immediate: there's no
      need to turn a casual chat into a pre-scheduled appointment
      or—worse—to sit waiting and wondering while those "dot
      dot dots" cycle like they do in a text interaction.

When employees tell us about their most memorable or impactful moments at work, we rarely hear about an inspiring Slack message or an MS Teams meeting that helped them see what they could become. But we *do* hear about powerful phone conversations, whether their manager was checking in during a difficult time, or just calling to offer some direct encouragement and praise.

2. "But younger generations don't like using the phone!" you're thinking. Let me tell you something, both from direct research and from my own experience as a millennial: that kind of age-based stereotyping will get you nowhere.

There are people in every generation who feel awkward on the phone, and there are also people in every generation who don't. A genuine conversation, a simple effort to connect one-on-one and see how a fellow human is doing—these are the moments that have resonated powerfully and profoundly with the employees we've interviewed, no matter what age group they belonged to. And that result is well worth the effort of ditching the typical work-communication channels and picking up the phone instead.

1 moment to master

I think you already know what I'm going to challenge you with this week. In fact, not just this week, but this moment! Do it right now: Pick up your phone, dial one of your employees, and create that moment of direct connection. You can offer some praise, ask how a project is going, or simply check in to see how things are going in their larger life. It may feel strange at first, but you'll be glad you made the effort—and it will get easier each time you do it.

6.3

3 SIMPLE WORDS EVERY EMPLOYEE WANTS TO HEAR

VIDEO 42

How to master the art of active listening

1 big idea

There are three little words that help every human being on earth feel connected, appreciated, and seen.

No, it's not *those* ones. It's: "I hear you."

2 insights from our workplace research

1. We all *think* we're great listeners, but we so rarely are. It's in our wiring to multitask, as leaders and as humans: while an employee is speaking, we're tracking the customers on the floor, the pinging on our phones; we're thinking about our next meeting or what we'll have for lunch (or—too often—what we're going to say when they stop speaking).

   Here's the thing: when you're not giving your full attention, your people *notice*. In our research, employees who felt disconnected from their work knew that their managers weren't listening to them: they could see it their body language, in their half-hearted responses, and in the fact that the needs the employees were expressing were not being met.

2. The leaders we meet who are able to maintain a high level of trust and connection with their employees practice active listening. They do this in three ways:

They take written notes

I'm talking pen and paper! This focuses your attention, physically *demonstrates* that you're listening, and even gives you a written record to refer back to.

They repeat back what they hear

Say back what you think an employee is telling you in your own words—and keep doing it until you're both sure you understand each other. This prevents assumption and miscommunication, and gives your employee a chance to clarify their needs.

They never jump in

Shutting up can be the hardest thing in the world! But often what an employee truly wants is a caring ear while they work out a problem for themselves. So listen first. Don't be afraid to allow a moment of silence before you speak. Then, before you launch in with your own solutions (as excellent as they are), *ask* if they are actually open to advice.

1 moment to master

This week, think back to a recent conversation you held with an employee, and revisit that interaction from their perspective. How do you think they experienced that meeting? If you weren't giving them your full attention, do you think they could tell? (*Hint: they could.*) And can you remember now what was said, and what steps you were each going to take?

Next, think about how that moment of connection might have been more meaningful for both of you if you had practiced the steps of active listening. And the next time an employee comes to you with an issue, take notes, listen before you speak, and repeat back what you hear until you have it right. Because your attention is one of the most valuable gifts you have to give.

6.4

YOUR OFFICE IS
STRESSING PEOPLE OUT!

VIDEO 43

3 ways to create a more functional workplace

1 big idea

Serenity. Breath. Mindfulness. If you see these words and dismiss them as trendy workplace woo-woo, you need to think again. Research is proving that what happens in your employees' heads and hearts is going to show up in your bottom line.

2 insights from our workplace research

1. Studies from Princeton, UCLA, and international workplace research centers galore have shown that clutter, digital disorganization, and other workplace stressors lead to lost productivity, wasted time, and decisional procrastination. Stress literally slows your employees down! And when we visit messy, unorganized workplaces, we see all that visual and physical chaos manifest in irritability, poor communication, and even mistakes. So de-clutter! As the famed Marie Kondo says, spark some joy!

2. Once you've cleared enough room in your workplace to think and breathe, you'll also be more free to *move*. You need this! Your employees need this! Our bodies are designed to move—and when they can't, they find all kinds of ways to let us know they're unhappy.

   If your workplace culture has your employees sitting in one place, hunched over a keyboard or cash register, eating lunch at their desk, emailing or messaging their co-workers when they could easily walk down the hall, then they're likely spending their days feeling achy, edgy, and physically stressed. But if you can foster movement—lunchtime walks, stretch breaks, stair-climbing competitions, even group fitness or yoga sessions—you can build a culture that's more relaxed, enthusiastic, mindful, and engaged.

1 moment to master

This week, identify the factors in your workplace that are stressing your people out the most—and then take action to reduce them. For this challenge, let your team take the lead: rather than charging in and throwing away everyone's favorite stuff, first go around and ask each employee what three everyday things in their environment are causing them the most stress or irritation. Listen to everyone's suggestions, and look for the themes that keep coming up, whether it's a depressing water stain on the ceiling, a sticky cabinet drawer, or a set of boxes that's always in the way. Then, boil all the responses down to the top five answers, and implement those suggestions right away.

6.5
WHY YOU NEED A "TO-DON'T" LIST

VIDEO 44

How a simple schedule creates better connection

1 big idea

Your employees have a different word for *mentorship*. They call it *time*.

2 insights from our workplace research

1. So many of the leaders we've worked with thought they had to pack their schedules with meetings, phone calls, emails, paperwork... and then a few more meetings. They ran themselves ragged—not because it was effective, but because they thought that "busyness" was a form of success. Or, at least, that it would be *perceived* as success.

   But our research shows again and again that the leaders who earn the highest levels of respect from their employees are the ones who are masters at keeping things simple. They create and protect space in their calendars to connect, to give their people access to them, or even just to think! It's not about shooting for lower goals. It's about giving everything you do—and all the people who do it with you—the full gift of your attention.

2. Clearing enough room for yourself and your people is a matter of setting priorities and creating boundaries. Call it your "to-don't" list. What inefficient tasks can you quit? What meetings can you say no to? What can you simplify, and what compulsive and unproductive habits can you shake—like checking email every two minutes, or scrolling your social media feeds?

If dropping any of that feels scary, think of it as a temporary test. Give it one week, if only to find out what kind of connection or inspiration might take root in all that empty space.

1 moment to master

If you're still convinced that busyness is necessary, find a few moments this week to ask yourself two questions. Here's the first: "When I come into work, how do my employees experience me?"

Can your people find you easily, and are you able to give them your full attention when they do? Are you *there* when you're there, or are you distracted and hurried? And question number two is even more important. It's this: "How do my employees experience *themselves* when they're with me?"

If you're feeling distracted, you're sending a message—whether you mean to or not. And your people will internalize that message: *I am a low priority, and I don't matter.* If you're feeling tired and burned out, they'll internalize that message, too: *My presence is a burden.*

If you don't like the answers to these two questions, start ditching some of the busywork you've been clinging to. Invest that time and attention in your people, and watch as the interest pays off in more connection and more loyalty.

6.6

THE PETTY CASH PRINCIPLE

VIDEO 45

How fostering "feel-it" moments can turbocharge initiative

1 big idea

Are your people free to seize the moment when they have an idea that could change a customer's day for the better? If you can't say they are, then it's time to give up the keys to the cash box.

2 insights from our workplace research

1. One of the most powerful moments we've witnessed in our research was the day an assistant at a dental clinic snuck out with a little petty cash.

   Why did she do it, and why was it great? Because a patient was completing a year-long chomper overhaul, and the assistant wanted to surprise her with a big bag of fresh corn. The dentist himself didn't know and didn't need to: he had empowered his assistant with the trust to spend some money and the freedom to leave her desk if the moment called for it. And when that patient came out of her final appointment and was presented with her favorite food? She cried at the gift, and at the realization that the assistant had listened and remembered.

2. Giving your people the tools and flexibility to act on their instincts doesn't just empower them to create meaningful moments for your customers—it helps them build meaning into their own lives too. As your employees experience the joy of acting on their ideas and

seeing those actions elevate others, they'll start to listen deeper, pay closer attention, and seek out more opportunities to create these "feel-it" moments. All you need to provide is a little bit of resources, and a whole lot of trust.

1 moment to master

This week, start building your own "feel-it" culture by leading with a few ideas, like a surprise customer discount code your people can offer when the time feels right, a stack of stationery to write personal notes to loyal customers, or a little stash of treats or gift cards to hand out on special occasions. As your employees start to take their own initiative, arm them with a petty cash fund they can use whenever the moment strikes. Once you've set that "feel-it" wheel in motion, you'll be amazed at the kind of creativity and caring you'll unleash.

MANAGEMENT MASTERCLASS SELF-ASSESSMENT

Module Review:
Mastering Your Moments Video 6

SECTION 6

Keeping the Main Thing the Main Thing

Part 1: Quiz

1. Your employees will best be able to engage with and support your company's vision statement if it is:

   a) Written in short, one-syllable words

   b) Brief, memorable, and authentic

   c) Punchy, powerful, and emotional

   d) Written in an AB rhyme scheme

2. True or false: An employee's age should not be your guiding factor in deciding how to communicate with them.

   ☐ True
   ☐ False

3. What are the three key elements of active listening?

   a) Nodding, eye contact, and a brief touch on the elbow

   b) Sitting still, maintaining an open posture, clearing your thoughts

   c) Relaxed face, body angled at 45 degrees, remaining silent until invited to speak

   d) Writing notes, repeating back what you hear, avoiding jumping in with a response

4. Name two actions you could take to reduce the amount of stress your employees are experiencing in your workspace.

   1. _____

   2. _____

5. As a mentor, one of the most powerful things you can offer your employees is:

   a) Time
   b) Oversight
   c) Friendship
   d) Competition

6. The "Petty Cash Principle" is about:

   a) Frequently buying small treats for your employees

   b) Setting up a test to see if you can trust your employees

   c) Giving your employees the means and freedom to act on their instincts

   d) Understanding that profit is not important in business

Part 1: Answers

1. B: Brief, memorable, and authentic (see lesson 6.1)

2. True: Your employee's individual personality and preferences (and your relationship with them) should guide how you communicate with them (see lesson 6.2)

3. D: Writing notes, repeating back what you hear, avoiding jumping in with a response (see lesson 6.3)

4. Any of: Get rid of clutter (e.g., remove old files, create open areas, bring in light and air), foster movement (e.g., promote face-to-face communication, hold step-count or other activity competitions, start a lunchtime walking group), promote mindfulness (e.g., host yoga or mediation classes, provide regular in-office professional massages, offer coffee alternatives) (see lesson 6.4)

5. A: An employee spells mentorship with T-I-M-E (see lesson 6.5)

6. C: Giving your employees the means and freedom to act on their instincts (see lesson 6.6)

Part 2: "Mastering Your Moments" Checklist

By the end of this section, I have:

1. Taken the "3-by-5 test" by attempting to write down my organization's vision statement from memory on an index card.

   GO DEEPER:

   ☐ Did you struggle to remember the statement correctly?

   ☐ How would your employees do at this test?

   ☐ Does your vision statement feel authentic to you? Why or why not?

2. Picked up the phone and made an unscheduled call to an employee to check in or to offer advocacy.

GO DEEPER:

☐ Did you feel anxious before making this phone call?

☐ What tools did you employ to push past any anxiety and act?

☐ How did you feel after the phone call was over?

3. Attempted to accurately recall what was said during a recent important conversation with an employee to assess my skills at active listening.

GO DEEPER:

☐ Were you able to remember what the employee wanted and what you agreed to?

☐ Would the outcome or actions that followed be different if you had employed active listening?

☐ How do you think that employee experienced that meeting?

☐ Did your employee trust you to follow through on what you discussed? Do they trust you more or less now?

4. Polled my team to identify and eliminate the top five stressors in our workspace.

GO DEEPER:

- [ ] Were you surprised by the types of stressors your employees identified? Were they similar to the ones on your own list?

- [ ] How resistant were you to the idea of reducing clutter?

- [ ] If you were able to create more open "negative space," how has that changed the dynamics in your workplace?

5. Created a "to don't" list of distractions and busywork I could stop doing to make more time for my employees.

GO DEEPER:

☐ How distracted are you in the workplace? How do your employees experience you when you speak with them?

☐ What unspoken messages do you think your employees are picking up from you in the way you interact with them?

6. Provided my employees with the two key ingredients of a "feel-it" moment culture: trust and an unlocked petty cash box.

GO DEEPER:

☐ Do you find it difficult to give up control and let your employees take action without first seeking your permission or direction? Why or why not?

☐ If you have established this opportunity, what kind of moments have your employees created? Did any surprise or impress you?

LITTLE BY LITTLE MAKES A LITTLE A LOT

7.1
WHY MANAGERS MUST BE OPTIMISTS

VIDEO 46

4 strategies for staying hopeful (while still keeping it real)

1 big idea

Successful leaders are optimists—they have to be! (Think about it: Who's going to rally behind someone who keeps saying it's never going to work?) But here's the good news: you don't have to be a natural-born jar of sunshine. Optimism can be *learned*.

2 insights from our workplace research

1. We live surrounded by bad vibes: stressful newsfeeds, Facebook arguments, sneering Reddit forums, bickering pundits. Optimistic leaders learn to tune out that constant rockfall of negativity. If you're struggling with pessimism, turn off Twitter for a couple of days. (Seriously! You will survive being offline for a while!) Disinvite yourself from that depressing Facebook group. Spend less time with people who grind you down with complaining, and more time with people whose presence uplifts you. You don't have to live in a bubble, but you can control what kind of noise you let into your head.

2. Being an optimist is not about ignoring the facts, or pretending the ride is easy even as your whole team struggles against the headwind. The leaders we've met who've steered their ship through bad times and came out the other side with a stronger team are always up front with their staff. But they also know how to show the hopeful side of the story.

If things are tough, say it. Acknowledge the challenges, the setbacks, the possibility of layoffs, or the risk of lost bonuses. Then say, "Look. These are the facts. But *this* is what we're going to do about it. Here are the possibilities if we stick to the plan." Don't make promises you can't keep, but do share a positive vision: "With determination, we'll find a new way to thrive. And we'll find it together."

1 moment to master

The first step to becoming more optimistic is to surround yourself with optimism. This week, conduct an audit of the voices and influences that are surrounding you right now, to help you identify the ones who could lead you to a more positive mindset. Make a list of all the people you actually connect with on a daily or weekly basis. Who among them seems to have the most optimistic mindset? Who always seems to express an authentically hopeful perspective on whatever situation they're faced with?

Next, think of a challenge you came up against recently, and try looking at that challenge through their perspective. What would their first thought have been? What hopeful pathway would they have been able to see when others were defaulting to fear or defeat? Keep meditating on that mindset, and start to view it as a sort of backup mental operating system—one you can switch over to when pessimism starts to creep in. Over time, you'll find that seeing the hopeful story can become genuine second nature.

7.2
FAIL YOUR WAY TO SUCCESS

VIDEO 47

Why great leaders have to mess up

1 big idea

So many managers refuse to try new things because they're afraid of failure. But ask yourself this: "If I don't grow and learn over the next five years, or ten, what will my leadership look like then? What kind of respect will I be earning if my knowledge and skills are a decade or more out of date?"

That vision of a stagnant future? That's what you should really be afraid of.

2 insights from our workplace research

1. Here's a weird thing we've come to understand about management: if you really want to succeed as a leader, first you're going to have to fail. A lot.

   Okay, yes: failure sucks. You know it, I know it, every manager we've ever interviewed has known it. But what separates the ones who stay stuck year after year, railing against the headwinds in their lives, from the ones who consistently earn respect, loyalty, and performance is whether or not they can accept and learn from their failures. If you can stay teachable, study your mistakes, and suppress the instinct to lay blame, then each failure can become a lesson—and another stepping stone to the future you want.

2. The leaders we've met who've had the most success with learning from failure went beyond merely accepting those lessons and actually adopted them into their character. How? By turning each lesson into a habit. First, you confront the mistake: take the time to think about what went wrong, what you should have done differently, and what learnings you should take from the experience. Then, grab your journal and write each lesson down in one short sentence or less. Review these lessons often, perhaps even saying them out loud, and make a note or a tick mark each time you realize that you've repeated a mistake or followed a new habit. This will help keep you on track, and cement those lessons into an ongoing practice.

1 moment to master

This week, sit down for a moment and think about all the mistakes you've made in your leadership over the last six months. After you've meditated on this for a couple of minutes, get a piece of paper and write down the top ten biggest failures that come to mind. (Can't think of ten, or any? Either you're a true unicorn, or you need to take a more honest look at yourself.)

_____

_____

_____

_____

_____

_____

_____

_____

_____

_____

_____

Now, review your list. Which one of those mistakes do you keep repeating, again and again? Which lesson feels the most powerful, or could lead to the greatest growth in your leadership? Choose one, and make that specific lesson your *mantra*—a keystone of your leadership vision for the year ahead. Write it down on its own piece of paper and keep it where you can see it every day. And never let that wonderful, valuable failure go to waste again.

7.3

ARE YOU HANGING OUT WITH THE RIGHT PEOPLE?

Why you need a personal board of mentors

1 big idea

Greatness demands a goalpost—and the same is true for leadership. If you want to be astonishing, surround yourself with astonishing people doing extraordinary things.

2 insights from our workplace research

1. No matter what industry we research, there's always one factor that separates the teams who love working for their bosses from the teams who don't. And that factor was not just any mentorship—it was the mentorship their leaders were getting themselves.

     The most admired leaders you can name all had mentors, even when they were at the top of their game. Sometimes they were hired for that role—like Bill Campbell, who advised and coached top C-suite talent from Larry Page to Sheryl Sandberg. Other times, they're simply a pool of wisdom to draw on: advisors, trusted peers, official and unofficial boards of directors. But whatever form it takes, no leader has ever achieved stratospheric success without that support and guidance.

2. What's important to remember is that you are being guided whether you intend it or not. Books, podcasts, talk radio, the way your peers in management talk around the office: these are all having an effect on how you think and who you are. So don't let that

development just happen. Take control of it, by hand-selecting your role models and influences. Consciously surround yourself with people you admire—whether that's your friends, the leaders you seek guidance from, or even the media voices you consume every day.

1 moment to master

This week's challenge is to take a hard look at the people who are influencing you right now. Who are the loudest voices that are surrounding you? Write down the top five (positive and negative), and be honest about it.

Now write down the top five leaders you *want* to emulate. (Define leader how you like: Colleague? Boss? Someone you follow but have never met in person?) Think about their values and the messages they send out to the world.

_____

_____

_____

_____

_____

_____

If your own values and the values of those who are influencing you don't match, then it might be time to turn the dial, change your habits, and start seeking out mentorship from a new kind of network.

7.4
WHY UNCERTAINTY CAN BE THE BEST FORM OF KNOWLEDGE

VIDEO 49

4 ways to maintain a teachable mindset

1 big idea

The more a manager learns about leadership, the more they realize how little they actually know. And guess what: that "not knowing" is actually a very useful strength.

2 insights from our workplace research

1. There's this sticky idea out there that great leaders have to be confident, authoritative, decisive—in a word, *certain*. But the truly great leaders we've met in our research knew that achievement isn't about complete knowledge, it's about complete teachability. As a manager, the worst kind of mindset you can get stuck in is to believe that you know better than anyone else.

2. The managers we've studied who've been the most successful at avoiding false certainty follow four simple principles:

   - They learn to embrace change, and to accept that what made sense in the past might not always make sense in today's context.

   - They remain curious, and approach each situation as a student, not an expert.

- They always accept offered advice with respect and gratitude.

- They redefine their understanding of ego by taking pride in their team instead of in themselves.

See, the world never stops, and as a leader you have to be able to move with it—maybe more so than anyone else. That openness, that lack of certainty, is a kind of managerial genius in itself.

1 moment to master

How teachable are you? This week, conduct a little audit on your reactions and approaches to new ideas, information, and even ways of being. Are you stuck in the belief that the old ways are the best ways? Do you—in your deep and secret heart—think that you're the only one who has the best answer to every situation?

If the answers to these questions make you feel uncomfortable—or if the very idea of answering them differently from how you want is frightening—just remember the words of famed basketball coach John Wooden: "It's what you learn after you know it all that counts."

7.5

STOP LOOKING AT YOUR PEOPLE AS A GENERATION

VIDEO 50

How age-based stereotyping is causing you to misdiagnose your workforce

1 big idea

If you really want to connect with your employees, stop trying to understand their generation and start trying to understand *them*.

2 insights from our workplace research

1. In our interviews, we so often hear a leader making massive generalizations to explain high turnover or low engagement: "young people today aren't loyal" or "millennials refuse to learn the ropes" or "Gen Z kids can't focus" or "twenty-somethings always think they know better."

    Diagnoses like these are based on assumptions instead of analysis—they're clumsy, dangerous, and can cause lasting harm. People born in the same decade do not magically share a personality (and what a boring world it would be if they did!). Some are driven, some are laid-back, some need structure, some like to follow their instincts—and the same will be true of any random selection of employees you could pick from any age group you want to name. Look at it this way: I bet you've met literally thousands of people from your own generation over the course of your lifetime. Were they all just like you?

2. If you want to reduce your turnover, you have to throw away those generational playbooks and diagnose your engagement and retention problems correctly. Don't listen to pundits, don't blindly follow culture trends—don't even do what I tell you to do if it counters your own direct experience with your people. Instead, shake off your biases and to get to know each employee as they are: their individual values, talents, and goals. Generalizations like "you should give millennials a games room" or "you should use TikTok to hire Gen Z" simply limit your thinking and blind you to what your workforce really needs.

1 moment to master

This week, I want you to really examine your own generational chauvinism and the stereotypes you believe about other age groups. Hey, let's be honest: whether we're Gen X or boomers or millennials, we can all fall into the trap of thinking our generation is the "best" one—the most capable, the most clear-headed, the only ones who really know what's going on. If you don't search out those beliefs and excise them from your thinking, they will doom your workplace to interpersonal clash and misdiagnosed turnover.

Remember: being the best *for* the world isn't about when you were born, it's about the actions you take and the standards you set for yourself. And since the attitudes you present are the ones your team will follow, that message of diversity and individual growth has to come loud and clear from *you*, the leader.

7.6

HOW TO RUN A MARATHON EVERY SINGLE DAY

VIDEO 51

Mastering mentorship in a million small steps

1 big idea
If the greatest part about leadership is that it matters, the hardest part is that it matters *every day*.

2 insights from our workplace research
1. Every musician understands that achieving genuine flow comes not from reading the notes but from internalizing the music. The craft of leadership demands this same kind of understanding. The managers we've met who had earned their people's loyalty were not *using* the principles of mentorship, they were *living* them. They knew that truly caring about your employees isn't something that just happens, it's a choice—one that you have to re-commit to every day.

2. If that sounds dramatic, it's not—and that's the real magic. We've seen that loyalty isn't built through big, flashy gestures and promises, it's built through small actions, made consistently over time. When we ask happy employees about what their manager does to earn their respect, we hear about moments of praise or encouragement, a bit of positive and helpful feedback at a challenging time, some advocacy for their talents and potential, and—more than anything—the feeling of being seen.

All of these actions were simple, but deeply profound. And if you pay attention, the opportunities to create such moments will arise.

---

1 moment to master

This week's challenge is actually a challenge for your full year ahead: I want you to put one foot in front of the other, and commit to making a tiny investment in your people every single day.

That's true advancement: small things, consistently, over a long period of time. With each step—today, tomorrow, and the day after that—you'll be creating connections that will have a lasting and powerful effect on who your employees are, and who they can become. And as you build purpose and meaning in their lives, you'll be building purpose and meaning in your own life as well.

7.7

WHAT MAKES A PICKLE A PICKLE?

3 ways to maintain your mentor management practices

1 big idea

Say you're a cucumber and you wanna be a pickle. You can't just shake a little salt on yourself once in a while and expect to come out different. If you want that change to be deep and permanent, you have to *stay in the brine.*

2 insights from our workplace research

1. Adopting a new habit is tricky. I bet you come across exciting or inspiring leadership strategies all the time, and each time think to yourself, "That's so great—I'm definitely going to do that!" But as much as you want to make that strategy a daily habit, after a while you just kind of... forget.

   Hey, forgetting is human! But we have seen that it *is* possible to carve a new path. You do it by automating your leadership: using your calendar, your phone, your alerts and alarms to actually pre-schedule those moments of mentorship and connection. If you're always waiting until the time "feels right," the advocacy and attention you need to offer as a mentor will never become a habit. Scheduling these kinds of moments is not cheating, it's conscientiously *changing*: those alerts and reminders will help you practice the principles of mentor management daily and methodically until they work on you at a fundamental level, the way a cucumber submerged in brine slowly turns into something new.

2. And there's one more amazing benefit to automating your leadership: the leaders we've met who practice this strategy are less damaged when they drop the ball. Think of it like watering a plant: if you do it every week—marking it in your calendar, setting out the can the night before, leaving yourself a note—then one or two gaps now and then won't do much harm. But *keep* forgetting, and that philodendron you love so much is going to wither, and it's going to get harder and harder to bring it back to life.

1 moment to master

This week, get out your calendar and actually pre-schedule a positive interaction with each employee under your direct supervision. Time an alert for each person, and when that ping goes off, don't hesitate: pick up the phone or walk over to where they are, and give them a moment of praise, advocacy, or attention—something personalized to who they are and what will have meaning for them.

It might feel uncomfortable the first few times—inertia and self-consciousness are powerful forces. But week after week, month after month, those moments of outreach are going to build trust, loyalty, and growth—in your employees and in yourself. That's your pickle, and that's change that keeps.

MANAGEMENT MASTERCLASS SELF-ASSESSMENT

Module Review:
Mastering Your Moments Video 7

SECTION 7

Little by Little Makes a Little a Lot

Part 1: Quiz

1. List two strategies named in this section that can help you maintain an optimistic attitude.

   1. _____

   2. _____

2. Your "personal board of mentors" are:

   a) The friends you gather with at 5 p.m. on Fridays to re-hash the work week

   b) The C-suite or owners of your organization

   c) A group of admired leaders you select to seek guidance from

   d) Your cats

3. True or false: Failure is part of success.

   ☐ True
   ☐ False

4. What are two of four ways to avoid false certainty (the Dunning-Kruger effect)?

    1. _____

    2. _____

5. A useful strategy for "staying in the brine" of mentor management is:

    a) Signing up for a fully immersive, all-inclusive leadership training retreat

    b) Giving an idea at least two weeks to "ferment" before acting on it

    c) Hanging pictures of strong leaders and role models from history around your office

    d) Using reminders and alerts to systemize and schedule your leadership

6. True or false: Millennials will always prefer an unstructured schedule.

    ☐ True
    ☐ False

7. The saying "little by little makes a little a lot" is:

    a) A reminder that progress is earned through small things, consistently, over a long period of time

    b) An effective response to employees who ask for a raise

    c) A reminder to avoid letting clutter build up in your office

    d) A business maxim coined by Henry J. Kaiser in in 1957

Part 1: Answers

1. Any of: Tune out negativity; focus on the good side of any situation; stay rooted in the facts; associate with optimistic people (see lesson 7.1)

2. C: A group of admired leaders you select to seek guidance from (see lesson 7.3)

3. True: Over the long term, lessons learned from failures are a necessary part of personal and professional growth (see lesson 7.2)

4. Any of: Learning to embrace change; remaining curious and approaching every situation as a student; accepting advice with respect; redefining ego by taking pride in the team (see lesson 7.4)

5. D: Using reminders and alerts to systemize and schedule your leadership (see lesson 7.7)

6. False: Making assumptions about any given individual's skills, preferences, or personality based on their age will only lead to workplace misdiagnosis (see lesson 7.5)

7. A: A reminder that progress is earned through small things, consistently, over a long period of time (see lesson 7.6)

Part 2: "Mastering Your Moments" Checklist

By the end of this section, I have:

1. Visualized myself as an optimistic person, and started practicing the four strategies for becoming more optimistic.

   GO DEEPER:

   ☐ Have you found yourself to be resistant to the idea of thinking in more optimistic ways?

   ☐ If so, why? What are you worried will happen if you choose to see and tell a hopeful story?

   ☐ Is there a difference in how your employees respond to authentic optimism as compared to either negativity or toxic positivity?

2. Made a list of my ten biggest failures from the last six months of my work as a leader, and the biggest lesson I learned from each mistake.

GO DEEPER:

☐ Which of those lessons have had the biggest impact on your professional or personal growth?

☐ How much of the resulting knowledge, experience, or wisdom would you have today if you had not made those mistakes?

☐ If you had read those lessons in a book, would you still have seen the same level of impact on your skills or leadership?

3. Made a list of the five leaders who have the biggest presence in my life right now (whether that's time, authority, or influence) and their top traits, along with a second list of five leaders I would like to learn from.

GO DEEPER:

☐ Do the traits from your current list align well with the "5 Cs" of great mentorship (confidence, credibility, competence, candor, and caring)?

☐ If any do not, what could you do to reduce the impact they have on your life and leadership?

☐ How could you start creating closer relationships with leaders who do embody the traits you would like to adopt for yourself?

4. Began practicing the four strategies for maintaining a teachable mindset: redefining my ego, embracing change, being curious, and responding to advice with respect and gratitude.

GO DEEPER:

☐ Do you often find yourself feeling threatened or defensive when presented with new ideas, practices, or opinions? Why or why not?

☐ What new ideas from the past were you uncomfortable with at first but have since adopted?

5. Interrogated any assumptions I may have about the individuals who work for me that are based on their age or generation.

GO DEEPER:

☐ Do you instinctively feel like your own generation has the most valid perspective?

☐ What about the people you know who are from a different age group—would they share that same generational chauvinism? Who is right?

6. Used my calendar or phone to set repeating alarms or reminders to reach out and create deposits of trust or moments of advocacy for someone on my team.

GO DEEPER:

☐ Do you struggle with the idea of "automating" your leadership? Why or why not?

☐ How likely have you been in the past to permanently adopt a new positive habit or strategy you learned about?

☐ How many such habits have you let drop?

7. Committed to the idea that leadership matters consistently, every day, in every small moment I design for my people and in every small deposit of trust that I make with them.

GO DEEPER:

☐ How has your leadership style changed since you began this Management Masterclass Series?

☐ What small action will you take today to invest further in the trust and loyalty of your employees?

☐ What kind of leader do you imagine you will be in five years? In twenty?

NOTES

1. Jake Herway, "Increase Productivity at the Lowest Possible Cost," Gallup, October 15, 2020, gallup.com/workplace/321743/increase-productivity -lowest-possible-cost.aspx.

2. Valerie Bolden-Barrett, "More Than a Third of People Admit to Lying on Resumes," HR Dive, January 17, 2020, hrdive.com/news/ more-than-a-third-of-people-admit-to-lying-on-resumes/570565/.

3. Work Institute, "2020 Retention Report: Insights on 2019 Turnover Trends, Reasons, Costs & Recommendations," info.workinstitute.com/ en/retention-report-2020.

4. "Inspirational Video—Be a Mr. Jensen—MUST WATCH!!" Clint Pulver, YouTube video, 3:12, youtube.com/watch?v=4p5286T_kn0.

Made in the USA
Las Vegas, NV
29 November 2022